Embracing the Exile

EMBRACING
the EXILE

Healing Journeys of Gay Christians

JOHN E. FORTUNATO

The Seabury Press : New York

1982
The Seabury Press
815 Second Avenue
New York, N.Y. 10017
Copyright © 1982 by John E. Fortunato
Printed in the United States of America.

Library of Congress Cataloging in Publication Data

Fortunato, John E.
    Embracing the exile.

    Bibliography: p. 133.
    1. Homosexuality. 2. Psychoanalysis and religion.
3. Homosexuality and Christianity.   I. Title.
RC558.F67   616.85'83406   81–21253
ISBN 0-8164-0508-5   AACR2

For Alison
A more loving guide
I couldn't have hoped for.

Contents

A Great Thanksgiving

I thank you, God, for Shelly Kopp and Lora Price and Sally Horwatt who taught me the rudiments of doing the work. Especially for Shelly who helped me to discover that being tough even when it seems cruel and being vulnerable even when it seems risky are parts of my job. The hard parts.

I thank you, God, for my patients, whose karma it has been to tolerate patiently all of my wrong turns and still graciously teach me what I've needed to learn.

I thank you, God, for Gerald May who dutifully harrassed me once a month to write "the next" chapter, who asked the right questions (the kind you despise when they are asked and appreciate later), and who, in the meantime, had the unmitigated gall to keep telling me that everything was just as it should be. Until I believed it.

I thank you, God, for my editor, John Ratti, who gently but firmly led me to understand that a "good" book is not a "perfect" book and that nit-picking is a compulsion of mine best not indulged.

I thank you, God, for Wayne Schwandt who ungrudgingly turned my original scrawl into a carefully typed manuscript and who put up with a full year of my ranting about the book,

avoiding it, and even saying it aloud. And then, in the end,
could reread it and be moved to tears.

And most of all, God, I thank you for my life. It has been
one hell of a trek. But I wouldn't have had it any other way.
Keep up the good work.

Love,
John

Preface

This book is an attempt to describe a journey of spiritual and psychological deepening for people who are both gay and Christian. It also looks at some ways that gay Christian people can be helped on that journey.

Some of this book is sheer storytelling. Some of it borders on professional theorizing. But most of it consists of musings—ideas, thoughts, and insights that I hope will be useful, both to those who help and to those who would be helped.

On the technical end, the helping relationship I present and illustrate will look suspiciously like insight-oriented, psychoanalytic psychotherapy. It is. The work I do is analytical in that it entails helping patients achieve insights about who they are and how they view the universe. The process involves analyzing with them at the most profound level possible their thoughts, feelings, and actions. It is a therapeutic journey because its goal is to enable patients to become more aware of who they are (as opposed to who they think they are), to see incongruities between who they are and how they live, and—if they choose—to make changes in how they live in order to achieve a greater sense of wholeness. People who have used their therapeutic journeys well feel more centered in the stream of their lives; they find life a more natural and meaningful undertaking.

But I would also contend that the work I do is different from traditional psychoanalytic psychotherapy in important ways. And I would contend that this difference somehow centers around the spiritual.

Technically, I don't know that there *is* a major difference between the work I do and what, say, an atheistic psychoanalytic psychotherapist does. We may, this hypothetical therapist and I, have been trained in different *schools* of technique; but, that aside, how we approach our work, the nuts and bolts of therapy, might well be identical.

What I believe would be different is the depth of our awareness, the scope of our universes. So I begin with a prejudice: that psychotherapy that does not include in its reality the spiritual dimension of human life is seriously lacking or deficient, lopped off, as it were, from its roots. What *spiritual* means in this sense will be unfolded in the course of the book. For now, suffice it to say that I believe that the work I do goes deeper than some traditional psychotherapy. It is my conviction that I frequently journey with my patients beyond the ego, beyond even the psyche. It seems to me we often tread on holy ground and glimpse together the face of God.

I am no maverick in this endeavor. Others before and beside me have sought to stretch psychotherapy to embrace the spiritual realm. The work I do and the words I use bear some resemblance to other approaches that incorporate spirituality into psychotherapy, like *transpersonal psychology, metapsychiatry*, and *yoga*. And, it would be impossible to proceed without mentioning Carl Jung who struggled his entire life with the psychospiritual dichotomy and whose followers push on to make the numinous aspect of life explicit in the therapeutic journey.

There are some who will be put off by my attempt. Just as there were many skeptics who scoffed at Jung for his interest in spiritual matters, so today, there are many scientific-minded practitioners who look askance at such "occult" pursuits. In some ways, the accident of history (Freud's having been a physician) that placed the "healing of souls" in the hands of the medical profession obscures, for therapists, our true ancestors: shamans, witch doctors, gurus, medicine men, and other spiritual "professionals" who were engaged in the healing of souls thousands of years before the advent of modern psychiatry. They have much to teach us.

This is not a book of technique. Having read it cover to cover, with no other training in psychotherapy or counseling, you will have come to know just enough about therapy to run a high risk of being sued for malpractice if it is all you use as a basis for your work. Those who would be professional helpers must be trained. No single book, let alone this one, is a substitute for that.

And this book is not the final word on counseling or doing psychotherapy with gay Christians. Although your interest in reading it may be to deepen your skill as a helper when working with gay Christians, I do not claim for a moment that it is *the* definitive text. There are some practical suggestions here, some attempts to establish a realistic context. There may even be some wisdom and truth. But there is no wish or attempt to be definitive. For those who would read on, I have included a fairly lengthy bibliography.

A final thing that this book is *not* is a how-to-do-it guide to spiritual direction. It is a ludicrous, though common, assumption that spirituality can be reduced to an intellectual discipline like theology or psychology. Spirituality defies such conceptual reductionism. Spirituality is not *about* anything. It *is*. Moreover it *is* everything. It *is* the journey, or at least the numinous aura around all of the journey. The only way to experience and learn about spirituality is by evoking or tricking ourselves into its presence through meditative practices, metaphor, the telling of stories, and other aesthetic media. Which is what this book, in part, is an attempt to do.

So the book ultimately is a journey. An experience. If you read it and grow, you will have deepened spiritually. But you will not necessarily "know" any more about spirituality. At least nothing you could verbalize conceptually or intellectually.

Which reminds me of a story. A patient named Tom came to see me with the following clear and succinct agenda. He had actually typed it up and handed it to me at the beginning of our first hour. First, he was having marriage difficulties. We would work on those. Next, he wanted to "work on himself," that is, he wanted to "get it together" psychologically. Finally, he had heard I was an expert in spirituality, and he wanted to deepen his spiritual self. He truly envisioned the journey as proceeding in that logically compartmentalized sequence. He was an attorney. That was the way he was used to doing business.

Tom wouldn't have understood if I had told him his therapy wouldn't progress in that fashion. So, naturally, I wholeheartedly agreed that he proceed as he planned. For a while, he drove himself crazy as he moved sideways through insights that were useful, opening, and growth-producing—but didn't fit his schema. Eventually, he gave up trying to make the journey fit his predetermined mold. But a lingering question remained. Periodically, he would ask plaintively, "But when do we get to the *spiritual* part?" I answered him variously. Sometimes I would say, "Ah, not for a while yet." At other times I would respond, "Soon. Very soon I think." Occasionally, in response, I would ask an unnerving question, "Spiritual part?" with a quizzical look on my face. "Huh! What do you think *that* would be like?"

During our first two years of work together, Tom deepened his awareness of himself and his place in God's universe immeasurably. He also made major changes in how he lived his life in the direction of just letting himself *be* instead of obsessively driving himself through the maze, as he had previously done. Toward the end of those two years, he was telling me during a session how much simpler his life seemed, how much more profoundly he felt that he belonged in creation, how much more he trusted himself to just be who he was, and how grateful he was to be alive. When he finished, I said, "Tom, what you've just said tells me how profoundly you've deepened *spiritually* during the past two years. I'm happy for you." He looked dazed, then scrunched up his face and snarled, "You sneak. We've been doing it all along! I thought it was something special." "Oh," I replied soberly, "but it *is* special. You've just told me *how* special."

Which belies my second prejudice. I do not believe that there is an exclusive, occult science called *spirituality* that is practiced *on* people. Psychotherapy *can be* a spiritual path, as can many other growth experiences. Any work, discipline, practice, course, relationship, or intentionality that opens a person to a broader and deeper awareness of the universe, any pursuit that helps people transcend themselves and begin to be cosmically conscious or united with God *is* a spiritual path. No technique, belief system, world religion, denomination, sect, or cult has the market cornered. Nor is any particular jargon or holy language or brand of God talk inherently more spiritual than any other. The journey is the journey. How its content is made concrete is, more often than not, incidental.

This book is only an attempt to help psychotherapists and counselors make the work they do a more effective spiritual path. If there is anything at all unique about it, it is its specific focus on work with gay people. Much has been written about homosexuality from a psychological, sociological, and theological standpoint. But almost nothing has been written that reveals the spiritual dimension of the journey of awakening for people who are gay. As a gay person, I can tell you how impoverishing that lack of written resources has been. If this book, in even a small way, directly or indirectly, helps gay Christians on their spiritual paths, it will have been a success.

Since this is a very personal sort of book, it seems logical to say something about myself so you know who is talking to you. First, I have already mentioned that I am a psychotherapist who is gay. For some, no matter what I say beyond that will fall on deaf ears. My credibility will have been shattered, my "otherness" having been established. Second, I have confessed my interest in the spiritual dimension of therapy. I presume that fact will alienate another group of potential readers. (I have just had this dreadful vision of books closing all around me.)

Well, for those who haven't tuned out, I will say that there is nothing remarkable about my credentials. Some seminary training in pastoral counseling, a graduate degree in pastoral psychotherapy, several years of clinical supervision with an assortment of psychologists and psychiatrists, an internship

at a state mental hospital, six years of personal psychotherapy
(in several lumps with two therapists), and about four years
of private practice. All rather ordinary.

My practice, too, is rather ordinary. I do psychotherapy
with individuals, couples, and groups, and my patients have
always been wonderfully diverse. The only thing that might
be remarkable about my practice is that approximately one-
third of my patients are gay males or lesbians. Which, now
that I think about it, may not be remarkable either.

Who is the book for, then? Well, since it is undoubtedly true
that authors write books for themselves in order to work out
facets of their own lives, the book is for me. It has been a way
for me to think more clearly about, and integrate, my own
sexual, psychological, and spiritual dimensions as a gay person. More, it is an attempt to begin to define for myself what
it means to do the work of psychotherapy.

I would suspect, then, that those who might respond most
fully to these thoughts would be other gay therapists, counselors, and spiritual directors who are making sense of being
both gay and Christian and who are helping others make sense
of it, too.

Next, I would guess, would be gay Christians outside the
helping professions who might find these musings helpful.
Since psychotherapy or spiritual direction are no more than
intensive opportunities for psychic and spiritual growth—en-
deavors that people have been engaged in for millennia in a
variety of ways—the healing journey described here can make
sense even if it is completely divorced from either a therapeutic or a spiritual formation setting.

The book is also for therapists, counselors, spiritual directors, or clergy of whatever sexual preference or religious per-
suasion who are willing to affirm gay people's sexuality as a
God-given gift, and, from that premise, try to help them make
sense of their lives. And the book is for parents and families
of gay people who wish to love and understand them better.

The book might also be of interest to modern-day healers
of souls who are mostly interested in the spiritual dimension

of the work, but are only minimally interested in the gay focus.

And finally, it is for anyone else: the curious heterosexual, the skeptical gay atheist, and any other seekers who are striving, with the same low batting average as me, I assume, to embrace *their* exiles, whatever shapes and sizes they may take.

:1
Once Upon a Time

Gay and Christian. Cornerstones of who I am. And, though it hasn't always been so, I've come to believe that *both* are good. Which has some immediate consequences.

First off, if "all good things around us" truly come "from heaven above,"[1] then my sexuality as well as my spirituality must be an expression of God's love for me. A gift. Love, expressed in a way that is me, must be from God, the Source of all love.

Next to contend with is a distinctive characteristic about gifts from God: you can't contain them. They want to be shared. Jesus encouraged us to respond to this tendency when he said, "The gift you have received, give as a gift."[2] He encouraged us even more strongly with the words, "When a lamp is lit, it is not put under the meal-tub, but on the lamp-stand where it gives light to everyone in the house. And you, like the lamp, must shed light among your sisters and brothers, so that, when they see the good you do, they may give praise to God in heaven."[3]

Once upon a time, all the giving and shedding of light came very naturally. It all flowed as it flowed out of a God-given, unselfconscious wholeness. It was all one: the universe, me, sexuality, God. Once upon a time, a time I can hardly remember, it all made sense. I must have been very young.

The whole world was a wonder then, including me. It all just was. There it was, just there, always ready to be wondered at, to be curious about, to be with. It was nice that way. I could just venture out into the cosmos and revel in it or fear it. Mud was wonderful stuff, and water, and sky, colors and textures, smells and sounds, people and bodies. They were all favorite friends. I liked words, especially. They were fascinating toys. And music. I loved music.

I could venture inward, too. And think about things. Explore things. My body, my mind, my imaginings. It was all just there. And there was nothing to do with it all but take in, be entranced by it, sometimes be terrified of it.

I went to Roman Catholic schools. Not just parochial schools, either. *Private* Roman Catholic schools. Academies. Small classes, lots of attention. In some ways it was nice. The nuns in private Roman Catholic schools weren't as crazy as the ones in the parish schools. There was more time to love.

There was good news and bad news about Roman Catholic school. The good news was that a few, real, life-giving spiritual seeds got planted in me. Some nuns really *were* holy. *Really* holy. They knew what standing in awe of the cosmos was about. They taught us with stories and pictures, by practice and example how to respond to our natural, childlike sense of the holy. The wonder.

A lot of it was kind of superstitious. Roman Catholics got carried away with symbols. Statues and relics, bread and wine. Everything got pushed a bit too far. Benediction of the blessed sacrament, kissing relics, kissing statues, God confined in that little box in the altar, the beads, the scapulars.

But it didn't much matter then. In a way, it was helpful for life to be oversimplified. After all, we were just kids. It was easier to grasp that God, the All in All, was in that little box or in that little circle of dry, cardboard-like bread than to try to take in the whole universe. The host was as good a focus as anything.

The important thing was that the nuns took it all seriously. I can still see the expression on Sister Mary Frances's face as she genuflected before the tabernacle. She was young, with lots of freckles. A pretty face, a little pudgy, blue eyes, small pursed lips. She smelled of Ivory soap.

There she was, enveloped in yards of black gaberdine, her face framed in snow-white buckram, her head swaddled in a meticulously draped black veil, her oversized wooden beads quietly chattering at her side. And as she sank down on one knee, her body erect and attentive, I glimpsed her face. It was radiant. No, honest-to-God, it glowed. As she gazed at the little, veiled box, she was transfixed. And so was I . . . by her face. I wanted it. Whatever it was that she had, I wanted it. It called me back to the wonder. I never wanted to lose it. God, she was holy.

That was the good news. The bad news was that she and I and the school and my parents all belonged to the Roman Catholic *Church.* One of those human institutions with all the warts or imperfections that human institutions seem held together with. And so, along with the seeds of spirituality a lot of weeds got planted, too. An awful lot of weeds. Mostly guilt weeds. And most of the guilt weeds had to do with bodies—*our* bodies.

"Temples of the Holy Spirit," they said. And of course they were right, but it was a con. Temples were supposed to be inanimate. You weren't supposed to *do* anything with them except hide them. Sort of like the veil on the tabernacle. Or the nuns' habits.

Bodies were shameful. Adam and Eve and the fig leaves. Like that. I remember one nun telling us never, *never,* to let on if we noticed that a woman was pregnant. Certainly never to *say* anything. It would be disrespectful. Being pregnant was very personal. Sort of like going to the bathroom. That seemed weird. I always wanted to tell pregnant women how beautiful they looked and to talk with them about how exciting it must be to have a baby in there.

Then there was "not *touching* yourself." Hell, you weren't even supposed to *look.* That was immodest. In fifth grade I went to a private Roman Catholic school just for boys. Some of us boarded; I was a day student. One night, just for fun, I stayed over at the school.

When it came to shower time, here were the rules: (1) To get undressed, you went to a corner of the dormitory and faced the wall. (2) You draped your bathrobe over your shoulders. (3) You stripped down, leaving your skivvies on. (4) You went to the shower room, took off your robe, *left your skivvies on,* and showered as fast as you could, *making sure* not to look at *anything.* (5) You went back to your robe and threw it over your shoulders, dried off, took off your skivvies, and dried the rest *making sure* nobody saw. (6) You went back to the corner of the dormitory and put your pajama bottoms on. (7) You threw off your robe and put the pajama tops on. (8) You jumped into bed. No exaggeration. Those were the rules. And everybody did it by the numbers. Or else. And we were only eleven!

You learned to be ashamed of your body early in Roman Catholic school. And, of course, my parents, being immigrant Italians, reinforced the whole thing. They had been taught well, too.

So things became confusing very early. I got the wonder, all right. But it wasn't supposed to have anything to do with bodies. God was out there somewhere, or in the tabernacle, or in here in your soul somewhere, but God wasn't in your body . . . or anybody else's body either. That was for sure.

Well, if that's how it was with bodies, you can imagine how it was with sex. Sex was a necessary evil. Period. The best option was to become a nun or a priest and avoid the whole thing. If you couldn't hack that, then you got married and had lots of babies.

I wanted to be a nun until I was seven. My mother finally convinced me that wasn't going to be possible, so she made me some minivestments, and I reluctantly gave up my veil for a chasuble. When I left fourth grade, everybody in my class was going to be a nun or a priest, except one girl. She was going to get married and have ten kids. She was considered a renegade, but what could the nuns say? It was legal. Not only that, she was the sixth of *twelve* kids. If they wanted the remaining six to go through the school, they knew better than to suggest her parents were oversexed.

A funny thing was happening with me during all of this. From about eight years old on, I sensed something was different about me. It had to do with my liking boys. But not the way you'd think. I wasn't like most seven- or eight-year-olds who hang out with boys because they hate girls. In fact, some girls were my best friends.

No, the difference was that I found boys attractive. I had no idea what that meant. Nobody ever talked about it. But there it was. Nobody knew *why* I chose Edward as my confirmation name at age nine. They didn't know that I had a crush on Ed Link, a sixteen-year-old greaser (1950s style) who worked on his souped-up Chevy in the garage next door. It wasn't just "older-kid" adulation, either. I was infatuated. I had erotic fantasies about him. When he would affectionately put his arm around me, I got aroused. Little did the unsuspecting bishop know when he smacked me on the cheek and said, *"Te confirmo, Giovanni Eduardo."*

Of course, I felt guilty. Homosexual tendencies aside, I had two strikes against me. First, it had to do with my body. Second, it had to do with sex. But this third thing felt really scary. It was hazy, but I knew it was awful. Maybe because nobody talked about it. At any rate, as programmed, I was ashamed of myself.

Things got worse. We moved to Boston from Philadelphia, and after one more year at a private Roman Catholic school, in seventh grade I went to a very W.A.S.P. private preparatory institution. Most of the kids were Protestant; quite a few were Jewish; there were only a handful of us Catholics. The gash between my spirituality and my sexuality was going to get much deeper during the next six years. The wonder took quite a beating.

I learned the word *homo* in seventh grade. Richard Kline and I were in the library, sneaking a look at some books of plates depicting nude Greek statues. He kept noticing the women; I kept noticing the men. It didn't seem remarkable to me until he remarked, a little amused, "Oh, you must be a homo." I was terrifically embarrassed. Although I didn't even know what it meant, the way he used it made it sound awful. But at least now I had a word for it. I looked it up in Webster's Second. It scared the hell out of me.

I got another taste of the fate that awaited me as a gay person that year. I got an erection in the locker room at school. I can't really remember what excited me, whether it was just being naked or whether I found someone there attractive (I suspect the latter). At any rate, there it was. I was still pretty naive; I didn't even notice.

A fairly sadistic upperclassman, a fat slob of a boy, caught eye of my excited state and invited a couple of his friends over for a look and a laugh. I blushed crimson (and quickly went flaccid) but he and his buddies tormented me for years about the incident.

The Roman Catholic thing didn't get any better either. Since I was in a non-Catholic school, I was packed off every Saturday to Christian Doctrine Classes. I had innocently been masturbating for a number of years by then, but I was soon taught that it was the worst sin you could commit (worse, by far, than murder or adultery or fornication). So began the long procession of Saturday afternoons, featuring the agony and overpowering sense of guilt as I knelt down in that dark little closet and whispered in ardent shame that I had "played with myself" five times during the past week. Then the harangues and condemnations and hours of penance. And you have to realize that I took all of this quite seriously. It was awful. I never did get up the courage to tell the priest what I had *fantasized about* when I masturbated. God only knows what the poor man would have done.

Week after week of guilt. An ever-increasing sense of not fitting. A slow, relentless rise of feelings that, somehow, *that* part of me was dirty, detestable, never to be acknowledged. I started getting disillusioned with Roman Catholicism; I thought I knew my oppressor. Sadly, since the wonder was tied to the Catholic, I was losing that, too.

Well, after the incidents in seventh grade, I learned quickly how to pretend. I became a closet dweller early. I dated girls. A lot of girls. I was half-considered a big man on campus, although I think most of my classmates "knew." But increasingly, *I* came to know I was gay. All my sexual fantasies were about men, mostly schoolmates. I fell in love with several of them. And I'm sure a couple of them felt the same way. But we could never do anything about it; we were all too scared. Unrequited puppy love. Some poignant tales to tell about "almosts" and "if we only could haves."

At fifteen, I discovered male pornography, quite by accident. I quickly got addicted to it; it became my only sexual outlet. At about that same time, my parents also started to "suspect." My mother rooted around in my room and eventually found my carefully hidden "mags." She never said a word to me. My mortified father and I, however, had a long talk, and then skulked off to the doctors. First came a hormonist and then a Freudian psychiatrist.

The psychiatrist began by telling me about electroshock aversion "therapy." Then he told me that, at my age, "these tendencies" were just a passing thing and that he wasn't too concerned. After hearing about the electroshock part I wholeheartedly agreed with him. And although he was the only nonjudgmental, supportive male in my life that year, in terms of my sexuality, we spent the next twelve months slinging the bull. Some good stuff I got from him, but not about sexuality. For this, my parents spent fifty dollars an hour. I've always thought that was poetic justice. In the meantime, I found a better place to hide my porn.

I ought to interject that during this whole period, I was beginning to get used to my gayness. Quietly, in the privacy of my room. Not that I liked that part of me; in fact, I hated it. But it was also becoming clear that that's how I was.

A year later (I was no longer seeing the psychiatrist), my mother found my stash of porn again. It must have been embarrassing. I think the plumber found it where I had it hidden in the basement underneath a bookcase next to a pipe that got stopped up.

But this trip was a little different. My father came into my room and asked me point-blank, "When do you want me to make an appointment for you to see *the* doctor?" Without hesitating a moment, I answered, "I won't go." "Do you know what this means?" he asked in alarm. "Do you know what this means for your life?" And again, without flinching, I said, "Yes." (I was lying, of course. I had no idea what it would mean to live life as a gay person. But I was tired of the b.s.) He tried to push, but I was intransigent.

He left, and soon enough my mother began one of her hysterical, crying, screaming, pleading productions, and I gave in. I went back to the psychiatrist. If only the man had not been burdened by his misguided neo-Freudian approach toward homosexuality, he would have been a godsend. As it was, we slung the bull for another year. Meanwhile, I found an ingenious place to store my porn, in the attic, under some floorboards. They never did find that spot.

And what about the church? The Spirit? The wonder? All just about dead. At seventeen, I had had it with the schizophrenia, at least *that* brand. I told my parents I wasn't going to church any more, that I was no longer a Roman Catholic. It felt like a matter of survival. But there was a stiff price to pay for surviving in my family. For starters, my mother didn't speak with me for two months.

Internal chaos, my senior year. Committable. Deep, deep depressions. Utter confusion. Hysteria. Going with a girl for show (I've come to think she was lesbian and it was a show for both of us). Deeply in love with the star of the football team. (I'm almost sure *that* was mutual. We would surreptitiously intertwine our feet for hours under the library table. Never could acknowledge above the table what we were feeling.) Church gone. Parents alienated. Psychoanalyst and me slinging bull. I almost flunked out. To this day I swear I graduated only by virtue of the headmaster's compassion.

The summer after my senior year, a breaking point was reached. My parents moved from Boston, while I stayed behind with a family we knew. The stated reason was to study organ at Milton Academy; the real reason was to get away from them. More survival.

There was a summer program at Milton that year. I got to know a few of the guys in that program and again fell in love.

Nothing happened. Again. All summer. The yearning became unbearable.

I remember one night, walking home across the football fields at Milton, home alone to this family's house, feeling so full in my heart and wanting so ardently to share that love with *someone*. The Milton man I had fallen for had just left for a party. And I wanted so much to be with him, intimately with him. To love him. Make love with him. And there I was, walking across that field, in the dark of night, so alone, so damned alone. And totally stuck.

I started to scream. I shook my fist at heaven and I cursed God. God, did I curse God. "God damn you, you mother-fucker!" I yelled. "Why are you doing this to me? I hope you drop dead, you sadistic son-of-a-bitch! You're not there! There's nobody there! I hate you! You *hear* that, mother-fucker God? I hate you! I hate you! I hate . . ."

I threw myself down on the ground, face up, and sobbed, screamed, and whimpered. I don't know for how long. A long time, I think. The last thing I remember whispering as I lay there was something of a prayer, "Please, God, if you *are* there, please send me *someone*. Please . . . anyone. Please . . ."

Well, nothing happened. No one appeared. And I guess I eventually picked myself up and walked home. I don't remember. But a significant change had taken place: I was an atheist after that.

And continued to be all through college. An adamant, disdainful, obnoxious atheist. You might think it would have given me the freedom to solve my sexual dilemma. Not a chance. I had buried the oppressor without; I didn't even know about the oppressor within. And I wasn't even close to accepting my sexuality as a gift.

I dated women some more. I had quite a reputation. Same script I had played in high school. I eventually got engaged to a beauty pageant queen. It had to be a *real* woman, you see. Then nobody would suspect.

I also had my first homosexual experiences in college. They were all awful, unfortunately. Except one. In one there was just a tad of real care and warmth. But mostly they were ugly, sordid, and dehumanizing. Which only added to my confusion and guilt.

As my betrothed glamour queen and I got close to the altar, I began freaking out. What the hell would I do in bed? I eventually went to the college psychologist to get "changed." After months of futile attempts, he finally levelled with me. "You know," he said, "I may be able to help you get comfortable being sexual with a woman, but you're probably always going to be a lot more attracted to men."

Initially, I was stunned. Then something clicked and I walked out. I walked out and broke off the engagement. I walked out resolved never again to do to a woman what I had done to her. I was gay. That was it. I wasn't ever going to try to be straight again.

So then what? What *would* I be? How would I *live*? The gays at Oberlin Conservatory made me very uncomfortable. Sibilants you could cut with a machete and mincing gaits that only Mae West could get away with. I wasn't *that*. What the hell *was* I? One thing I was still sure of, though: the pain and rejection that I knew I would face if I "came out" was more than I could bear.

I needed a rest. Since I was flunking a good number of my courses, withdrawal seemed like a good option. I signed up for the Peace Corps, a decision with which my draft board disagreed. They won. First year at Fort Knox. Second in Vietnam. Sexually, the army meant for me two years of celibacy. Spiritually, though, some surprises were in store.

Having been an organ performance major at Oberlin, I always ended up playing in churches, conducting choirs. Sacred music. Always just for the money, of course. Church was a joke. But for an atheist, I was often the most regular churchgoer in the crowd. Funny thing, huh?

While I was in Vietnam, I became close friends with the chaplain's assistant. Just an accident, you understand. Business. Organists have to coordinate with chaplain's assistants, etc. Right.

Gerry was a Church of Christ minister, wrestling with the confines of his own denomination, as it happens, but undeniably Christian. We frequently talked long into the night, although seldom about religion. He never *ever* challenged my atheism. But I don't think he ever believed it, either. He just dropped a few subtle, pseudophilosophical questions here and there. The sneak. They would bear fruit later. And of course, in the meantime, he and I were busy planning services for the chapel, picking hymns, going out to the field to bring God to the boys on the front. Some atheist I was.

With Bronze Star on chest two years later, I returned to Oberlin very distracted. I was much more intrigued by Gerry's questions than ontological relativity. By "accident," I slipped and broke my left leg in seven places two weeks into the semester. How happy I was when the surgeon solemnly declared that I would have to withdraw from school again.

I spent seven months sitting. I couldn't walk at all, except to get from here to there. There was much pain, but there was also much growth. A lotus position it wasn't, but immobilized, there was nothing to do but turn inward. I'm imagining readers murmuring, "It was about time." You would be right.

My organ professor came to visit me every Thursday. He was a caring, loving person. Also a very conservative, midwestern Episcopalian, which stood in stark contrast to the radical, East Coast atheist I had become. But he came every Thursday afternoon for seven months and sat with me. God bless him.

He, too, was wrestling with religious questions. We would swap books, devour them, and talk. For hours.

During those seven months, I read *all* of C. S. Lewis, most of Teilhard de Chardin, the whole New Testament, and a smattering of other things.

I don't know how it happened. But, like C. S. Lewis, I was "*surprised* by joy." Slowly. Undramatically. But those spiritual seeds planted so many years before in private Roman Catholic schools began to sprout. A conversion experience. No question. By the end of the seven months, I had reclaimed my sense of wonder. I was a believer. A born-again believer. In love with the universe, I was. It wasn't nonsense to talk about God any more.

It was both a gift and a dilemma. A gift because the joy was deep and rapturous. A dilemma because, in many ways, I was back in the mud again, only mired even deeper. What was I to do with this *and* my sexuality?

You have probably begun to perceive a seesaw pattern in all this. A spirituality-sexuality teeter-totter. A rather unsettling oscillation. Reject one, lift up the other. Reverse. Reverse. Affirming a piece of myself while denying another. Lifting up both or even imagining that they were part of a wholeness called *me* remained unfathomable. How far down a crazy-making, self-splitting path I had stumbled from that primordial time when all was one. Well, back to the story.

I hadn't finished with flailing myself around. Roman Catholicism was all I knew. It was Holy Mother Church. When my spiritual seedlings started to grow, I only knew about being a Roman Catholic. So I went back. I confessed to a young priest that I was gay. He told me God loved me *anyhow*. Gay was sinful, but God loved me anyhow. He gave me absolution. It was still screwed up, mind you, but it was sure as hell better than before. It was a strange liberation.

I became devout. Mass every morning. Reading the divine office. Teaching Sunday School. And it was no mind game. I was spiritually nourished as never before.

I eventually decided that the thing to do about dealing with my new-found spiritual depths and my repressed sexuality was to sanctify them. This time I would bury my genitals in a monastery. It would solve everything. I would get affection and friendship and spiritual nourishment, I thought, but be celibate. I started shopping for orders.

I had transferred by this time to Ohio University. There I met a Carmelite friar named Tom, an older, fatherly man, a zany guy, whom I came to love dearly. He enticed me into the Carmelites.

If all Carmelites had been like Tom, I might still be one. But religious orders were going through turmoil in the late sixties and early seventies, and the monastery I was sent to in Washington was a hotbed of confusion. None of my expectations were met. As far as affection and friendship were concerned, there were almost none. (We were called the ships that passed in the night.) And, in the wake of Vatican II, the house was composed largely of theologically angry young men who were inclined to reject *everything* ever put out by the Roman Catholic Church. Habits were silly. Obedience was passé. And poverty? We had the best-stocked bar in Washington, a stereo system that would have made any audiophile perk up and listen, eight cars at our disposal, and more spending money than I have ever had, before or since. It was a religious fraternity house. What's worse, there was virtually no prayer in the house; some people didn't even feel it important to go to community mass on Sunday. So there I was, emotionally starved, spiritually starved, *and* celibate. It was the driest period of my life to date.

But the Lord provides. A brother from another house and I fell in love. This time I was ready to act on it. As a jovial and enlightened older brother later said, we "eloped." It was to be the first time that I would actually have to grapple with *being* gay, *living* gay, *out* at least to me and him.

Well, neither of us were *proud* of being gay. So we eloped to the wilderness of southern Maryland. Granted, there were two of us now, but it was to be two of us in a double-bed closet. We exiled ourselves, hoping that we could be off somewhere, quietly out of sight, out of mind. It was really only a little less schizophrenic than before. But as with my seven-month journey toward embracing my spirituality, those three years with my friend in southern Maryland allowed me to begin embracing my sexuality. It was an uphill climb.

In the process, we almost did each other in. They were sometimes strifeful years. But we managed at least to begin *being* gay, being in a gay relationship, living with a gay person. *And* to be Christian.

We got involved in Dignity, a caucus of gay Roman Catholics, and in the Metropolitan Community Church, a Christian denomination that predominately serves the gay community.

The rift between spirit and sexuality began to be healed. Very tentative, very conflicted. But it was a start.

Our relationship ended precipitously, and there followed for me another agonizing and crazy year. I left southern Maryland, moved to Washington, got more involved in Metropolitan Community Church, also got involved with a few men, and then met a special man named Wayne whom I married and with whom I spent the next five years of my life.

When I moved to Washington, having had to grieve the loss of a four-year lover all by myself in the wilds of southern Maryland, I was resolved never to be in the closet again. So when I took a job, I planned to be out. And I was. I started slowly, coming out to only a few people. But by the time I left that job, everyone knew. And few cared. It was a pleasant surprise. I thought I was safe.

Wayne's and my relationship deepened, blossomed. We knew we had found something special. We were awed by it. We recognized it as a gift—from God. It was a healing time.

Our church community at the Episcopal church of St. Stephen and the Incarnation in Washington, D.C., a kind of crazy, renegade, progressive parish at that time, embraced our love for each other. They wanted to literally *celebrate* it with us. A service, a union, a covenant, a marriage. Nobody knew what to call it. But it was to be a time of lifting something special up, blessing it, and publicly affirming it. That's when the trouble started.

With tremendous naïveté, we greeted the larger Christian community. Our sisters and brothers of the faith—and many outside of it—listened but didn't respond quite the way we expected. The planned service got a lot of press, something we neither expected nor desired. We thought this was just going to be a service for our community.

The publicity opened up a hornet's nest of hate. Hate mail and obscene phone calls, condemnation by a conclave of bishops, and tirades from a few theologians. I was called everything from a corrupter of children to an abomination; psychotic, a deviant, an aberration—and worse! The local bishops declared *ex cathedra* that the planned service would

bring ridicule and disgrace on the Episcopal church and for-
bade it to take place, threatening this and that if it did. I lost
my job. My family abandoned me. And it soon became clear
that there was a substantial silent minority of our parish
community that hadn't liked the idea of who I was, who *we*
were, or what we were doing, at all. They left.

All in all, short of physical violence, all of my worst fears
during all of those years in a closet came true. It was awful.

The service did take place—somewhere else. And I suppose
it was wonderful, as services being held under siege go. I was
too much in shock by then to really be there. The joy had
been pretty well laced with bitter herbs.

The publicity and notoriety went on for some time. Television appearances, radio, newspaper features, speaking en-
gagements. I had become what is called in the gay community
a professional faggot. But through all the hype, I felt myself
withdrawing. I wanted out. It was all crazy.

I remember one night in particular. I got up in the middle
of the night, leaving Wayne in bed. I went and sat in the dark
in the living room, smoked too many cigarettes, and rocked
in the recliner. And I meditated, I guess you'd say. I pondered
the whole mess in my heart of hearts.

It all welled up. All the doubt, the pain, the outrage, the
hostility and hate, the rejection. All of my brokenness. I sat
and rocked and cried and raged. And I waited. Waited for
something. Some insight. Some revelation. Something to help
me get out of the mess I was in. I think I rocked a long time.

Slowly it all began to drift away—all of the insanity, all of
the pain—I kind of went numb. And then I had a vision. I
know, that's crazy. "Woogie" as a friend of mine would say.
It was all my imagination, right? Well, maybe it was, but I
had a vision. I imagined something.

I imagined I was sitting there and God was sitting there,
too, on the couch right in front of me. It was very peaceful
and dark. But I could see him. He was bright. We were talking.

I was saying, "You know, sometimes I think they're right,
that being gay and loving a man is wrong." God smiled and
said quietly, "How can love be wrong? It all comes from me."

But I was a wreck, you'll remember. It was going to take more than that. "Sometimes, I just want to bury that part of me," I said, "just pretend it isn't real." "But I made you whole," God replied. "You are one as I am one. I made you in my image." I knew he was trying to soothe me, but I had just been through four months of good Christian folk trying to cram down my throat that I was an abomination, so all this acceptance was just getting me very frustrated. So I tried again. "*Your* church out there says that you don't love me. They say that I'm lost, damned to hell." "You're my son," God said in a way both gentle and yet so firm that there could be no doubt of his genuineness. "Nothing can separate you from my love. I redeemed you before the beginning of time. In my Father's house, there's a mansion waiting just for you." I started to fill up. "What do I do with all this?" I asked, weeping now and clenching my teeth—at my wit's end trying to have it all make sense. "What do I do with *them*?" And in the same calm voice, God said, "I've given you gifts. Share them. I've given you light. Brighten the world. I empower you with my love. Love them."

That did it. After all I had been through, I had had it with sweet words. Who was he trying to kid? I pounded my fist in exasperation and cried, "*Love* them? What are you trying to do to me? Can't you see? They call my light darkness! They call my love perverted! They call my gifts corruptions! What the hell are you asking me to do?"

My words echoed in the silence. My breath stopped. It felt vaguely like eleven years before when I had lain on a football field at Milton Academy and cursed the God who sat before me. Only now it was different. Now he was *here*. Now I believed. God, was I scared.

There was silence. God didn't move a muscle, though his gaze was much more intense. And with a voice filled with compassion, a voice that enveloped me with its love, God spoke.

"Love them anyway," he said. "Love them anyway."

:2
The Cleaving of the Soul

I n one sense, the preceding story is specifically about me. It is an actual slice of my life. And I doubt if many gay Christians can relate to the particulars. Most have probably never come out in *The Washington Post*, or been married in a controversial Episcopal service, or flailed themselves around with quite the panache I've managed to exhibit. I am ready to admit that I'm crazy. For some gay Christians the pain of their journeys may have been greater; for some much less. Their story lines probably go very differently. But my guess is that the major components are common to us all.

The denial of our gayness for some period. The questioning of our faith. The seeming irreconcilability of our sexual and spiritual selves. The schizophrenia. The feelings of unworthiness. The guilt. The loneliness. The hiding. The closets. And the sense of being on the fringes, cut off, banished. The story within the story belongs to all of us who are gay.

To be gay and Christian, integrating both into the wholeness we deep down know ourselves to be, to embrace them both as gifts of God, and to live our lives authentically, rejoicing in those gifts as part of the uniqueness that makes us who we are is to place ourselves on the outskirts of the community we most care about. It's beyond the realm of choice. Exile is simply where we find ourselves when we are who we are. It's most often a hard place to be.

Banished. We come bearing gifts that aren't welcome. We come with love to give that's rejected. Outcasts, "despised and rejected of men," driven to the desert, or at least to that rather desolate ribbon of land that keeps the desert at bay from the arable land most people inhabit.

God's charge is to all of us, too: "Love them anyway." Loving anyway. Sharing anyway. Giving gifts even when no one wants them. Embracing the exile. It demands a profound belief that not only can "life on the fringes" be endured by gay Christians, but that being banished can be viewed as an incredible spiritual opportunity. To give and love while all the while being disdained as "the most abject of people" gives us such distinctive lamp stands on which to perch our lamps that, when our sisters and brothers see the light we emit and the good we do, they may even *more* profoundly give praise to God in heaven.

Loving in the face of utter rejection means following in some of the most painful footsteps of Jesus, the Christ. But I'm convinced that peace is to be found in accepting that calling—not peace in the everyday sense of *tranquility,* but the kind of peace that emerges from believing in our wholeness and the rightfulness of our place in the cosmos. Loving in the face of persecution may not always yield happiness, but it seems to be the only response that allows us to make any sense at all of our lives.

For gay Christians to be able to love, give, and find meaning in a world that rejects and isolates them, the cruel gash separating their sexuality from their spirituality must be healed. Their freedom to love and give in a hostile world hinges upon their coming to believe in their wholeness and in their having a rightful place in God's universe.

But there is a more primitive brokenness to be healed first, a brokenness of which the gay Christian's spirituality-sexuality dilemma is only a subtheme. A brokenness that also explains much of the current craziness that permeates Western society and that helped create the gay Christian's dilemma. It has to do with the contemporary view that people are split into parts—into psyches and spirits.

The segregation of the human soul into psychological and spiritual dimensions is a fairly late and predominantly West-

ern invention. Shamans, witch doctors, medicine men, sor-
cerers, miracle workers—even priests in the early Christian
church— were simply healers of people's souls. No distinction
was made between mind and spirit; all human nonphysical
ailments were considered disturbances of the soul and were
thought to be caused by demons or evil spirits or to be divine
retribution for sinfulness.[1] In the East, by the way, the distinction between mind and spirit is hardly recognized at all.

How we came to view the God-given unity of our souls in
two parts is a complex psychological-sociological-anthropol-
ogical phenomenon. There isn't space to deal with it here.[2]
But it happened. During the past 75–100 years especially, we
came to accept as fact a rigid compartmentalization of our
nonphysical selves into psychological and spiritual components.

In the psychology department, Freud gave us his analytic
construct of intrapsychic forces and dynamics. Then there
followed Freud's disciples who elaborated on his model, and
his detractors who replaced it or changed it out of recognition.
And we are still living in an intellectual climate in which
post-Freudianism and anti-Freudianism are rife. If the psyche
was to be enhanced or healed there was analysis or psychotherapy or, more recently, encounter groups, and now T.A.,
est, Lifespring, and other manifestations of "pop" psychology.

Our spiritual selves, on the other hand, were theoretically
under the care of Holy Mother Church, which provided nourishment or healing through Sunday worship, the sacraments,
devotions, doctrine, law, Bible study here and there, and, for
the more rigorous, an ascetic life as a cloistered nun or monk.

Slowly, the psyche-spirit rift is being debunked.[3] And it's
happening mostly because both sides have felt something
missing. Psychology has been straining at its confines, trying
to grow beyond its dimly perceived limitations. And spiritually starved people have been leaving the church in droves,
frequently looking to the East for more deeply rooted ways
to acquire spiritual nurture. In the process, some have begun
to wonder whether psychotherapy and spiritual formation
aren't, in fact, the same journey.[4] They are different systems
and have different jargons, to be sure, and different convic-
tions about "the meaning of life." But both seem to be pulling

in the same direction, and both seem to want to deal with the same general area of a person's being.

What is common to both pursuits is the goal of heightened awareness or consciousness. Both the psychotherapist and the spiritual director want those in their care to come to know more, experience more, and be more consciously aware. Both try to help the people they see professionally gain *some* kind of "enlightenment." But there are differences. And those differences revolve around the question, "What are people to become enlightened about?"

Psychotherapy concentrates almost exclusively on raising patients' *self*-consciousnesses. The therapist's job is to help patients better understand the inner processes of their minds. They're also supposed to help patients learn to control those processes and achieve a sense of self-determination and autonomy.[5] The analytic center of the universe is the patient's psyche.

The theoretical assumption is that people have at their disposal innate, real power (ego strength) that is theirs to unleash if only they can shake off the intrapsychic shackles that bind them. Exercising the ego is supposed to yield happiness.

In analytic terms, a mentally "sound" person looks like this: a "healthy" (strong) ego at the center, flanked and complemented by the superego and the id, all present in a context in which the patient is consciously aware of what he's experiencing and why he's doing whatever it is he's doing.

And the model is useful. Through the intrapsychic focus, patients *do* resolve a lot of their inner turmoil. Damage done to them in childhood and adolescence can be repaired. Impoverishments or distortions of their "maps of the universe"[6] can be explored and corrected. The roots of behavior that alienate patients from other people can be dug up, pruned, and new behavior adopted. People get a lot of help in traditional analytic therapy; a substantial amount of integration and healing can and do take place.

But in comparing it with spiritual formation, there are two important things one should notice about the analytic mindset. The first is the tenacious focus on the intrapsychic arena.

The second is the supremacy of the conscious ego as the epitome of mental wellness.

Spiritual formation is also concerned with heightened awareness, but isn't at all interested in self-determination, self-control, or autonomy. What spiritual seekers are after is called *atma* in Hindu philosophy, and *atma* is usually translated as "enlightenment." *Atma* describes a mode of being in which there is awareness of "the all." It is pure consciousness, unattached to self—unattached to anything—with neither thinker nor object of thought, neither see-er nor seen. Pure, cosmic consciousness. It's a state of just simply being.

There is a Christian counterpart to this Eastern formulation. Christian spirituality is grounded on belief in the infinite power and love of God and the nothingness of humankind, the cosmic oppositeness of Creator and creature.

The goal of Christian spiritual formation is "union with God."[7] This Western equivalent of *atma* envisions nothing short of total forgetfulness of the self and complete surrender to God, a replacement of the ego—the autonomous, self-determined self—with God's presence. Emptying ourselves of our delusional sense of power, we make room for the only power that is real, the power of the Holy Spirit.

Contemplation, the practice of spiritual growth, brings us face to face with the overwhelming everythingness of God: immortal, all-knowing, all-wise, all-loving, all-merciful, all-powerful, all-yielding. Contemplation means trying to truly stand in the presence of this God who is All in All. If we succeed, we cannot help but experience our emptiness, powerlessness, and infinitesimalness.

> Who are we that you should be mindful of us,
> Mortals that you should care for us?[8]

The experience of this cosmic oppositeness leads us to surrender, giving up everything to God.

What can we say, now, about the differences between psychotherapy and spiritual formation? What are people to be enlightened about in each? And what can we say about the so-called components of the human soul?

The vision of the psychotherapeutic journey is clearly limited to enlightenment of one's self *to* one's self. The focus is on the psyche. The spiritual journey, on the other hand, envisions transcending one's self and becoming open to and one with God or the Mystery or the cosmos. For Christians, at least, the focus is on God.

Stated this way, it looks like psychology and spirituality are two legs of the same journey. You would seem to begin on the psychological path and then continue along the spiritual path.

But there happens to be a paradox involved in the interface between psychology and spirituality that makes things more complicated. Oddly enough, the psychological portion of the journey seems to focus on strengthening the ego, whereas the spiritual part clearly envisions giving it up. If they are legs of the same journey, it is a very strange journey: the legs are going in opposite directions.

Well, it *is* a strange journey and the paradoxical relationship is for real. If both aspects of a person's soul are to be tended to, the journey becomes something of a tug of war. Healing requires tearing. Psychospiritual growth is a process of gaining control and giving it up, of acquiring ego strength and then surrendering it. Sometimes it is a dramatic flip, as when a sociopath [all ego] turns saint [all God] (Paul on the road to Damascus?). More often, the journey entails an upward back and forth rhythm in which each increment of self is first affirmed, then transformed into God. Whether you're a yogi proceeding upward through the seven chakras or a Trappist monk climbing *The Seven Storey Mountain*,[9] the journey involves grasping onto, then letting go of chunk after chunk of the self.[10]

Visualized like this, spirituality and psychology seem more like integrally connected, parallel aspects of the same journey. A visual aid that's been useful to me in understanding "how it looks" is a double helix, rather like a DNA molecule. One strand of the double spiral represents the psychological or ego dimension; the other strand, the spiritual dimension. Like the DNA molecule, there are a series of links between the two strands. Also like the DNA molecule, the strands are twisted; it's a torturous journey.

There is at least one drawback in this visual analogy. Unlike DNA, the two strands of the psychospiritual journey are not equal in either strength or intensity. The dominant strand is the spiritual one. The journey's progress is initiated on the psychic strand as some chunk of the ego is affirmed, and then achieves fruition by jumping across one of the links to the spiritual strand, as that chunk of ego is transcended. The directionality, then, aside from the upward progression along the double helix, is always *from* the psychic strand *to* the spiritual strand.

Is doing the work involved in the psychological dimension— acquiring a sense of autonomy and self-determination—a prerequisite for spiritual growth? I think it is. I'm convinced of the wisdom of those spiritual masters who contend that "you have to have an ego before you can give it up." Eastern disciples have to rail against their gurus and attempt to maintain control before they can arrive at the insight that there is nothing to control. Likewise, Christian seekers have to gain some feeling of self-worth and power before surrendering to the everythingness of God. Otherwise, there is a danger that the "surrender" may end up being nothing more than a self-deprecating reinforcement of a negative self-image. Reinforcement of the self-image—whether positive or negative—just yields a more powerful ego. It isn't spiritual fruition at all.

The Western split between psyche and spirit is false. For either to make sense they have to be seen as inextricably intertwined aspects of the same journey. But we have lived with this divorce for a long time. And I am contending that it has made us crazy. I am also contending that it is the root of the gay Christian's dilemma. It is time to substantiate those claims. And to do that, we must begin by looking at how this schizoid view of the soul has been externalized in our view of the world.

:3
The Enthronement
of the Ego and the Myth

Regardless of how psychology and spirituality got separated, we can assume it was no accident. Nor is it an accident that during the past 100 years psychology has waxed while spirituality has waned. If we viewed the estrangement of psychology from spirituality as a battle, could we doubt which was the victor?[1]

Psychology's ascendance marks the enthronement of the ego. It isn't a coronation that only took place in Western society; it's been fairly generalized. But the ego's reign in the West is especially autocratic. Its current reign, divorced from spirituality and ignorant of its natural directionality toward spiritual transcendence, is a serious distortion of reality. Using the double-helix image, what we've done is to ignore the spiritual strand and proceed up the ego strand as though that's all there were.

Perhaps the most striking manifestation of the enthronement of the ego is a pop psychology experience like "est" whose philosophy centers around "personal power." "I can do whatever I like." "I can get whatever I want." "The only thing keeping me from getting what I want is that I don't believe enough in my *self*." And so on.

The "est" philosophy, it seems to me, is living proof of the logical absurdity of what happens when psychology is divorced from spirituality. The ego runs wild. "Esties," especially right after graduation, are so often characterized by unbridled aggressiveness, unflinching self-centeredness, and mind-boggling grandiosity that it has led a colleague of mine to coin the phrase "post-est megalomaniacs." Frankly, I find them scary.

But est is just one dramatic example of an egocentric distortion in world view. Egocentrism is the basic philosophical stance of all of Western civilization as we know it. It has become indomitable in the United States.

The basic dilemma of an egocentric world view is this: with the ego planted firmly at the center of the universe, what do we do with all of the multitudinous data of human experience that constantly remind us of our powerlessness? If we choose to look, it smacks us in the face. In the face of a universe whose dimensions are almost incomprehensible, how grandiose can we be? How in control of nature are we when faced with a tornado or earthquake or tidal wave? How powerful are we when, in an instant, an accident or natural disaster can snuff out our lives? The evidence of our powerlessness surrounds us. But if you need to think you're absolutely in control, what do you do with all that evidence?

The answer is that you block it all out. Which brings us to what I call *the myth*. Put succinctly, the myth is the tenacious belief that we really *are* in control of ourselves, our destinies, each other, and the world. It gives rise to mythologization, the construction of a society of systems and structures aimed at guaranteeing our continued, undaunted progress up the ego strand of the double helix. Its job is to ensure that nothing is given over to the spiritual strand and that all of the possible links from the psychic to the spiritual strand are severed. The myth underwrites our egocentrism.

In order to better understand this myth—why we think we need it, and how it affects our lives—it may be helpful to take a slight detour. If we approach it by looking at the reasons why people go into psychotherapy or study yoga or seek spiritual direction, we may get a clearer picture of what the myth is trying to avoid and how it goes about avoiding it. After all, both psychotherapy and spiritual formation are intense, painful journeys. Why would people choose to endure either path?

Are there similarities between why people decide to submit to the torturous journey of psychotherapy or subject themselves to the unrelenting purgations of a guru?

Spiritual students' dissatisfaction with life is usually generalized. By whatever turn of events, they have become acutely aware of an uneasiness at the center of their being, a basic insecurity that never goes away. Alternately, they experience a sense of being called forward, a yearning to grasp something more profound about life. German philosophers have called this uneasiness or yearning *angst*.[2]

The word *angst* literally means "anxiety," but the philosophers aren't referring to the day-to-day anxiety that life brings. They are talking about the deep sense of restlessness that is part and parcel of being human. They point to the human experience that, no matter what we do, being human always feels like not being "at home."

We want, sometimes desperately, to have "gotten there"—to be complete—but we seem always to be in process, becoming, incomplete. If we dare to look, to sense, and to acknowledge, we realize that there is no place in the universe where we truly fit, where we belong. Strangers in a strange land, consigned to wait, to search, and never quite to find the answers to the ultimate questions that would make sense of life.

In contrast with this yearning that is the common experience of those who seek the spiritual path, patients in psychotherapy usually want help because of a specific problem. They want relief from symptoms: depression, loneliness, anxiety, anger, suicidal tendencies. These are what drive patients to a therapist. Unlike spiritual students, patients generally aren't aware of the angst that underpins their "problem." And whether or not they ever see past the symptoms to the angst depends on whether the patient stays interested in the journey once the symptoms disappear. It also depends on whether therapists perceive their role any more broadly than that of relieving symptoms. Whether or not patients acknowledge its presence, though, the angst is there, and, ultimately, it is the root of their problem, as we'll see in a moment. The common element in people's motives either to start down the spiritual path or to go into psychotherapy is angst. For either, the pain of their life situation has gotten bad enough to lead them to decide that they must do something specific about it. As hard as either therapy or spiritual formation may seem to them, it promises to be less intolerable than continuing with things as they have been.

Most of us decide early on that the whole pursuit—whether psychological or spiritual—is just too deep, too hard, too long. Psychotherapy is for people who are "sick"; spiritual formation is for the esoteric. Most of us can "make it" on our own.

But the angst of the human condition presses upon us just the same. We are constantly surrounded by reminders of our powerlessness and of our human fraility. The angst just sits down there, gnawing at the pits of our stomachs. We want it to go away. We want to *make* it go away. But how?

We begin by clinging tenaciously to our egos. We *are* in control. We are *not* powerless. We then take the denied, buried anxiety and project it onto the world about us. "Out there" in the world, we create for ourselves a myth. And an elaborate myth it is.

We create in our world systems and structures that we can manipulate and control to somehow bury the reality that we truly control nothing. Our never-ending strivings to control more and more of the universe are responses to our equally perpetual, denied sense that we are helpless in the face of a cosmos whose power overwhelms us.

We spend our lives nurturing our systems and structures, making them "work for us," as people say. Economic systems, systems of government, family systems, cultures and subcultures. Budgetary systems, data systems, social systems, communication systems, and exhaust systems.

There are promotions to grub for, benefits to grab, social strata to climb, bigger houses to expand into, more power to amass, and more things to buy.

And then we take out insurance to underwrite the whole edifice. Health insurance, life insurance, car insurance, disability insurance, and Federal Deposit Insurance. Pacts, treaties, and settlements. Backup systems, second teams, and alternate plans.

Conglomerating these structures, we create global macro-systems: the World Bank, NATO, the World Council of Churches, the United Nations, the International Monetary Fund, and multinational corporations.

We also create microcosmic systems: philosophy, mathematics, science—even biblical exegesis, and the incredible number of carefully circumscribed specializations in each of those disciplines provide examples of our ability to explore, manipulate, and, we hope, control the most minute portions of our experience.

Notice that the purpose of the whole house of cards is control. Our mythic world is a world of naming, conceptualizing, defining, fixing, circumscribing, defending, protecting, insulating, isolating, preventing, and aggrandizing. It is all ego. All aimed at reassuring ourselves that we are powerful, self-determined selves.

For most of us, dedication to and elaboration of the systems and structures alluded to by the litany above take up a lifetime. The striving is consumed; insecurity and angst are kept at bay; the myth is preserved.

Let's look again, now, at why people go into therapy. We have observed that most people enter psychotherapy because they are troubled by symptoms. They hurt. They sense that "something isn't right."

There is another way to say that now: most people go into therapy because some part of the myth isn't working for them. Something in the system has malfunctioned and the angst of the human condition has broken through. Death, serious illness, family discord, divorce, separation, and job loss are some of the more common precipitants for entering therapy. They are all instances of mythic system breakdown. The symptoms—alcoholism, addiction, loneliness, nervousness, rage, withdrawal, depression, anxiety—are all outward and visible signs of the inward and denied angst. They are all reminders of how fragile the mythic house of cards really is.

Because we have braced ourselves so resolutely against experiencing our angst and the reality of our powerlessness, when precipitous events occur in our lives, they overwhelm us. We "can't cope." We become immobilized. We go to see a "shrink."

Most often, what patients want when the system breaks down is relief from the resultant pain. But the way they usually see this happening is by getting back into the mythic system, reintegrating themselves into it either by shopping for a new system configuration or by changing their behavior so that they "fit" in the current configuration. They believe that relief from their symptoms will come if they can only change enough to get reincorporated into "society." Why is this so?

Well, for the myth to work, everybody has to believe in it. Children are indoctrinated into it from infancy on. Belief in its reality is reinforced by schools, colleges, and all of our other social institutions. It governs every aspect of our lives. Adherence to the myth is a must, and sanctions are applied against recalcitrants. (Can you imagine the vice-president of a multinational corporation suggesting to the president that the latest planned merger is really unnecessary because they're powerful enough already and, besides, it's really all a game?) The myth demands that it be taken seriously. Patients coming to therapy, then, automatically assume that there is something wrong with *them*. "Society" is assumed to be basically good, healthy, constant, and reliable.

This is nothing new, of course. Analytic theory was founded on the philosophy that since it is the patient who is uncomfortable, it is the patient who must change. Insanity traditionally has been defined as some people's inability to fit into society. Mental healing came to mean, then, helping patients change so that they fit into a given world. Only lately has this view begun to yield.

Insofar as patients buy into this mythical view of society as normal and themselves as eccentric, their goal will be to renovate themselves. And, often enough, psychotherapists end up fostering just this kind of renovation. Mental illness is to be cured. Family discord can be made harmonious by family *systems* therapy, loneliness by encounter groups, feelings of powerlessness by assertiveness training, anxiety by stress management training, and hostility by scream therapy. The goal of many therapies is to help patients adopt new mythic behavior.

The problem is that this view of society is a fairy tale. "No, Virginia, society really is not good, healthy, constant, and reliable." But we have come to think we need this fairy tale to underwrite the more fundamental unreality that human beings are inherently powerful, or, in other words, that exercising the ego—individual or collective—is the core of human living.

Frequently, people who undergo therapy whose primary goal is ego building and societal reintegration leave "feeling better," at least for a while. They go off into perhaps a different part of the maze than they were in before, but they go into the maze nonetheless. The striving is consumed; the insecurity and angst are once more put at bay; the myth is preserved.

:4
The Gay Predicament

W hen I started working with gay people, I was struck by the number of ultimate questions they asked. Questions like "Why me?" or "Why is life so hard?" erupted during moments of sheer desperation in therapy. Those eruptions happened often.

A session with a patient named John is an example. John was twenty-four, attractive, blond-haired, and blue-eyed. He had grown up in a rural Michigan county. Although nothing about his visual appearance was stereotypical, he had a few mannerisms that some might interpret as gay. Nothing dramatic. He crossed his legs at the knee instead of at ninety-degree angles. He held cigarettes between the last knuckles of his index and middle fingers instead of nestling them in the crook between. He just wasn't terribly particular about performing usual, unconscious actions in ways generally prescribed for American males.

We were five weeks into the therapy and John had spent every session recounting incidents about how badly he had been treated as an emerging gay person. From adolescence on, the relatively subtle mannerisms, coupled with a lack of interest in organized sports and an avid interest in theater and art, reaped for John a nightmare of ridicule, harrassment, and physical violence. He was the chief object of mockery in school from junior high through high school. For both peers and faculty, he was a constant butt of humor. Once, while in a restroom, he was stripped naked by a group of boys and his clothes flung out the window. His locker was regularly rifled and his books stolen. On two occasions, he was sadistically forced into performing sexual acts with his male—supposedly heterosexual—peers. One of those times was at knife point. In other words, he was raped.

During this entire six-year ordeal, his family not only gave him no sympathy, but harrassed him themselves. His brothers treated him almost as brutally as his classmates. His father was so disgusted with his "faggot son" that he hardly spoke to him. And his mother, a fervent fundamentalist Christian, almost daily subjected him to evangelical tongue-thrashings about how he had better change his ways and repent or be damned. The only thing approaching solace John got during his entire adolescence was some half-hearted pity from a younger sister who admittedly thought he was weird but still felt some kind of kinship with him.

Week after week, I listened to gruesome anecdotes, as John unfolded the horror for us both to see. We alternated between weeping and railing as years of fury and anguish were played back. The tape seemed endless.

At the end of the fifth session, as he finished pouring out the details of an incident in which his father, drunk, had beaten him almost to unconsciousness, screaming that he would rather have a dead son than a gay son, John stopped, with face contorted and fist clenched, and screamed out, "Why me?" "Why did I have to be gay?"

I didn't answer. There *was* no answer. He knew it. And after a silence that seemed like forever, he buried his head in his hands and sobbed. He sobbed for a full twenty minutes and I held him as a mother would hold a terrorized child. A mother he had never known.

"Why me?" "Why is life so hard?" "Why did I have to be gay?" "Why do people hate me because I'm different?" "How can God love me?" These kinds of questions have punctuated my work with gay patients from the beginning.

To take a traditional analytic approach, and view such expressions as "manifestations of intrapsychic conflict that needed to be resolved," was absurd. I began to hear them as spiritual questions—cries into the abyss, desperate pleas for meaning. And it was through those questions that I began to realize how important exploring and nurturing a gay patient's spiritual dimension was in therapy. I wanted to know why spiritual nurturance was so important for gay patients. More than that, I wanted to learn how I could better provide it.

Why gay people needed more attention paid to their spirituality wasn't obvious to me at first. After all, I thought, the situations that catapult gay people into therapy aren't very different from those that propel straight people through the door: death, serious illness, separation from or difficulties with a lover or spouse, the loss of a job, family problems, addiction, loneliness, and hostility. The stimuli for seeking help all seemed about the same.

The keys to understanding the difference were the intensity and unresolvability of those painful life situations for gay people. Two examples will illustrate this point.

Four years ago, I was working as a technical writer for a small software manufacturing firm in the Washington area. By anyone's standards, I was successful at my job, was given more and more responsibility, and, after a year, received a substantial promotion.

Also during that year, almost all of the other employees came to know I was gay. We would be chatting about domestic affairs or what we had done during the previous weekend and, as people talked about *their* spouses, I would talk about *mine.* There wasn't anything forced about my "comings out"; it just happened naturally in the course of conversation. Much to my surprise—braced as I was for rejection—it never made a bit of difference. My gayness wasn't an issue for my co-workers. I got along well with all of them.

One month after I was promoted, my spouse and I were involved in the rather well-publicized marriage ceremony I described in Chapter 1. My employer was livid; he asked for my resignation. Since he'd just promoted me, I refused to give it to him. I pointed out that my being gay had no impact on my effectivity, nor was it causing any difficulty with other employees, nor did my activity in the church have any connection with my job.

But he was resolved to get rid of me. He began a conscious and cruel regimen of harassment aimed at forcing me to resign. I was stripped of all supervisory responsibility, put under the thumb of a man ten years my junior, moved from office to office, and finally located next door to the owner himself who used the proximity as a way to torment me further. Accusations of tardiness, abuse of the telephone, and so on, all unsubstantiated, became a daily diet. My attempts at dialogue or reconciliation were met with stony resistance. He wanted me gone and wasn't going to rest until he got his way.

He finally won. I resigned. There just came a time to count up my losses and move on. I left a high-paying position in which I had performed well and worked congenially with co-workers and clients, without a ghost of a chance of using that part of my employment history as a reference.

Qualitatively, the loss of a job on nonmerit factors simply because someone is gay is different from being fired during a political coup or because of a cutback or for incompetence. Of course gay people aren't the only ones who suffer the effects of discrimination in employment; blacks, Hispanics, and women have felt it, too. But at least there are now laws that try to protect these other minorities and provide some mechanism for recourse. As with other minorities, being fired from or harassed out of a job simply because of *who you are* is hard enough. Having no recourse places the victim in an unresolvable predicament. How do you get closure when there's no way out?

But employment isn't the only area in which gay people face a unique brand of rejection. It permeates their family lives as well. Other minorities can at least expect to be supported in regard to their minority status by their families, especially in the face of discrimination. A black family certainly isn't going to reject a daughter who is proud of being an Afro-American. An Hispanic family isn't going to abandon a son who is being treated badly at work because of his ethnic background. But gay people face probable rejection here, too. They usually end up being isolated on both fronts.

There is a haunting story in Howard Brown's book, *Familiar Faces, Hidden Lives*,[1] about a young man named Tim. Tim was twenty-two. He had become active in the gay rights movement in college, but hadn't yet come out to his family. During a special television report on gay liberation, Tim spoke. It ended up on the evening news and his parents were watching.

> Before Tim's next visit home, for his sister's sweet sixteen party, his parents had questioned his brother and sister and concluded that they had a "fag in the family" after all. When he appeared at the party, his father remarked: "Son, if you want to be queer as a three-dollar bill, that's your business." Tim walked away without saying a word. Then his mother approached him. She put her arm around his shoulders. Tim took this to mean that she was going to accept him. "Tim," she said, "I've made only one mistake in my life." Tim asked her what she meant. "Twenty-two years ago," she said, "I should have had an abortion." Since then, Tim's mother has taken to telling neighbors and friends that he is dead. And Tim's father speaks to him as if he were a complete stranger when Tim calls to speak to his sister or brother.[2]

Disownment or rejection by family—often the norm for gay people—is different from family turmoil revolving around an adolescent's adjustment at puberty, or a daughter who, at twenty-two, is trying to cut the umbilical cord, or a son who is about to marry a woman his parents don't like. It's different because, unlike these other situations, it's not how a son or daughter is *acting* that's being rejected, it's who they *are* constitutionally. They don't have a choice about being gay, there isn't anything inherently destructive in their sexual orientation, and yet, once found out, they are treated like lepers by the people who supposedly love them the most. How do you get closure when there's no way out?

These are just two examples of the kind of rejection gay people face. Chapter 8 will take a much closer look at the oppression of gay people and how it affects therapy. What needs to be emphasized for now is that, unlike other minorities, gay people, if they are honest about who they are, are likely to be rejected across the board. Parents, siblings, friends, employers, the church, children (if they've been heterosexually married)—all are more likely than not to reject them.

Some may say—even in the gay community—that I'm exaggerating, that things are changing, that they know gay people who *have* been accepted by parents or friends or employers. And that's true. I know some of those people. And there are gradations of acceptance as well. Gay people living in cities suffer less social isolation and rejection than those in rural areas. Gay people in the arts suffer less job discrimination than those who attempt management careers in industry. Children of progressive, educated parents are less likely to be rejected than children of immigrant, blue-collar worker parents.

As for things changing, I'm not so sure. In some ways, things have gotten better for gay people. But the rise of right-wing America and the reactionism they are about makes me wonder if things won't get worse before they get better. For right now, change seems stymied.

When all's said and done, I think I will stick with my earlier contention. Generally speaking and all things considered, the plight of gay people in American society is pretty bleak. More often than any of us would like to admit, the isolation gay people usually encounter *is* of the magnitude illustrated above.

The kinds of frustrations that land both gay and straight people in therapy, then, are very much the same: family difficulties, job insecurity, marriage problems, loneliness. The intensity of those frustrations is often much greater for gay people, but in a way, that's irrelevant. What *is* relevant is that gay people most often are unable to resolve those frustrations in the ways straight people do.

Using the concept of the "myth" described in the last chapter, we can put it this way. Both gay and straight people end up in therapy usually because some part of the myth isn't working. They have spun off from their galaxy of systems. That experience creates anxiety and they want relief from it. For the gay person as well as the straight, the hope is for reintegration. But here the similarity ceases. Gays are blocked from reintegration within the mythic system. They are stuck with their frustrations. That's the gay predicament.

I recall a patient who came to me with the following list of goals that he wanted to achieve and integrate. First, he was gay and, for the sake of his self-esteem, wanted to be *out*, all the way out. Specifically, he wanted to be on the cutting edge of the gay rights movement. Second, he lived with a lover who was very much in the closet, who wanted to stay there, and who felt his closet was being threatened by his gay militant mate. This was causing a lot of domestic strife that my patient wanted relieved. Third, he wanted to be a Roman Catholic priest.

Now were the patient straight, with a similar configuration of goals and problems, things would have been very different. Say, for instance, a patient was a civil rights activist and needed to speak publicly on the issue. And let's say that he was living with a woman and was fulfilled in that relationship. Let's suppose, too, that she was protective of her privacy, wanted none of the activist limelight, and that his continued activity was causing considerable friction between them. Finally, let's imagine that he, too, wanted to be a Roman Catholic priest.

There isn't any way to know how therapy would go with this second, hypothetical patient, but for the sake of demonstration, let's imagine how he might work things out. He would start by exploring, letting go of, and getting past the old and current material as well as the neurotic behavior that got him into this mess. Once free of those shackles, this straight male activist might decide (1) that his woman lover was entitled to her privacy—that he could be public on whatever issues were important to him, yet share the rest of his life with her; (2) that he might be an Episcopal priest instead of a Roman Catholic one, and not have to deal with celibacy;

although (3) he might have to marry the woman to be an acceptable candidate for Episcopal Holy Orders.

That is, of course, grossly simplistic and ridiculously condensed. Therapy *never* goes that smoothly. But, admitting the oversimplification, what we have just done is to have deciphered a way in which the man could buy back into the myth and be fully integrated into some set of the myth's systems.

What should be obvious is that for the gay patient presented earlier, not only is the myth not working, but it isn't *going* to work, probably for the rest of his life. To try to achieve and integrate the goals he expressed in therapy through action in his life would create for him untold havoc and unresolvable frustration.

It is nearly impossible to be a gay activist and have a lover who is in the closet. Even if the relationship were presented to the world as "roommates," the world would be hard-pressed to believe that the secretive partner was straight when he lived with a roommate who was a gay activist. Second, no Episcopal or Roman Catholic bishop is likely to ordain an openly gay activist to the priesthood, let alone invite him to share a rectory with his lover! In short, there isn't any way this fellow can achieve and integrate his life's desires that, for a straight man in a similar context, might well be possible.

Some might argue that straight people are just as able to paint themselves into corners and come up with life ambitions and desires that are just as unattainable. "I want to make a million dollars and not work." "I want to cheat on my wife and have her remain faithful to me." Or—an example provided by a mentor of mine—the case of his retarded deaf-mute patient who really wants to be an astronaut but will settle for managing the Orioles. Logically, that argument holds water.

Maybe the difference *is* only quantitative. Maybe it's just that the shackles placed on gay people are so much more binding than the normal restraints placed on straight people. What other group of people can be imprisoned for ten years or more for simply engaging in private, consensual sexual acts with another adult? What other minority can be arrested in a bar their minority frequents and be hauled off to jail for "loitering"?

Most of all, maybe the difference has to do with the goal of being honest—out—combined with almost any other goal: reaching a management position anywhere in the Fortune 500, living with a spouse or lover in the suburbs or country, becoming an ordained minister, teaching school, enlisting in the armed forces, becoming a child psychologist, working in a gas station, joining a police force, or being a professional athlete. Or this assortment: being married in a church to a same-sex spouse, adopting children, being able to dance at a nongay disco, or simply feeling free to casually hold hands or kiss goodbye in public without being arrested or harassed. The list is endless.

The life options of an openly gay person are so limited that, although the difference between them and those placed on straight people may *logically* be a matter of degree, the experiential difference is qualitative. It isn't just a few increments of difference; it's more like a quantum leap.

The fact is that American society is bulwarked to prevent gay people from getting in. Most of the mythical systems and structures, conventions and customs, which heterosexual people use to allay their angst and keep their sense of human powerlessness at bay are off-limits to homosexuals.

What happens to people who are excluded from the myth? There they stand, face to face with the angst of the human condition, wanting desperately to escape through the same hatches that everybody else is using, but the hatches are locked.

Ultimately, they get depressed. They may run from it for a while, escaping into some part of the strange, wonderful, and convoluted minimyth that the gay subculture offers. And they may get angry for a while and grow bitter at the injustice of their life situation. But sooner or later, they get depressed. Very, very depressed. Often suicidal. It is when they reach that rock-bottom place where there is nothing to do but drink the oppression to the dregs that gay people are thrust down to their spiritual roots with a force only oppressed people can understand. Faced with the full impact of human angst and no way to escape, they shout angrily and terrified into the abyss, "Why me?"

It is no surprise, then, that either right from the beginning or as the therapy progresses, gay people ask an inordinate number of spiritual questions. Either because they realize it when they come to therapy or discover it in the process, they come to grips with the frightening reality that they must give up the myth *forever*. Since their progress up the ego strand of the helix is blocked, the only choice they have is to jump to the other strand. Whether or not they consciously grasp their yearning as a need for spiritual grounding, the cry into the abyss is an acknowledgment that the only way *out* is *deeper*.

Simply transforming a negative self-image (spawned by whatever the patient's history included) into a positive one is just not enough when you're going to send the patient back out into a world that is determined to slash those feelings of worth to shreds. Surviving and growing in such a world demands that the gay person develop a perspective much larger than the societal myth itself—a spirituality much more profound. The process of therapy with many gay people, then, has got to involve awakening in the patient levels of consciousness far beyond those necessary for most straight people.

What does all of this have to do with "loving anyway"? In order for gay people to get to a place where they can love in a world that rejects both their loving and giving, they first have to embrace a consciousness that transcends the society that rejects them as misfits, a cosmic wisdom that comprehends the oneness of the universe in which the gay person inextricably "belongs." The psyche-spirit split must be debunked and the myth abandoned. Once you know, at the core of your being, that you have a rightful place in God's creation, that nothing can separate you from the love of God, then it doesn't much matter what people say or do to you. Then you are free to give and love—anyway.

Gay Christians have a good many forebears on this journey. Our exile, though different in the specifics of time and place, is the same as those of many other groups who have had to endure banishment for the sake of their faith. It helps a little to look back and see that we're not alone. It is also useful to look at our forebears' journeys and glean whatever wisdom they picked up along the way. The most meaningful ancestral journey I think gay people can look to for guidance is that of our Hebrew forebears who were exiled to Babylon after the fall of Jerusalem in 587 B.C.[3]

When Jerusalem fell and the temple was destroyed, Israel's false, nationalistic faith in a God who would protect them no matter what they did crumbled. Many Jews gave up their faith entirely. They began worshiping other gods, especially the Babylonian gods who apparently had proved their superiority. Others began to worship the god of wealth, capitalizing on their new location in "captivity" to nourish their greed. Still others clung to the hope that the Davidic state, the theocracy complete with priesthood and temple, ritual and sacrifice, would be restored.

Through all of this confusion, the Hebrew faith, amazingly enough, did not die. But it changed dramatically.

The scriptures written during the exile are marked by denial (Lamentations 5:7), rage (Ezekiel 18:2, 25), and forlornness (Psalm 137). Israel at first could not accept the idea that God would let this thing happen to them. Once it seemed inevitable, they were overcome with bitterness directed at their captors. Finally, they were immobilized by sadness and hopelessness as their fate seemed sealed. But, toward the end of the exile, a new voice arose, the voice of someone we do not even know, someone who wrote what scripture scholars call Second Isaiah. And his writings begin this way:

> Comfort, comfort my people;
> —it is the voice of your God;
> speak tenderly to Jerusalem
> and tell her this,
> that she has fulfilled her term of bondage,
> and her penalty is paid; . . .[4]

Second Isaiah was a herald, a herald of something new, a herald like Moses or so many of the prophets or John the Baptist or Jesus. He announced a broader understanding of God's plan for the universe, and he witnessed to a spirituality whose depth had never before been realized.

Second Isaiah came to understand the universality of God. Yahweh was no longer just the God of Israel, but the Lord of All, a cosmic God.

> Who has gauged the waters in the palm of his hand,
> or with its span set limits to the heavens?
> Who has held all the soil of earth in a bushel,
> or weighed the mountains on a balance
> and the hills on a pair of scales?
> Who has set limits to the spirit of the Lord?
> What counsellor stood at his side to instruct him?
> With whom did he confer to gain discernment?
> Who taught him how to do justice
> or gave him lessons in wisdom?
> Why, to him nations are but drops from a bucket,
> no more than moisture on the scales;
> coasts and islands weigh as light as specks of dust.[5]

With this broader view of reality, the Israelites could begin to see their way out of the mess their nationalistic theology had gotten them into. If God was Lord of All, then everything had a purpose, everything fit. Simplistically, Cyrus could be seen as God's pawn sent to overcome the Babylonians and effect the release of Israel from bondage. In a more sophisticated way, the exile could be seen to have a purpose too: to purge God's people, renew their faith, and unify them so that they could become God's servant, God's Suffering Servant.

> I, the Lord, have called you with righteous purpose
> and taken you by the hand;
> I have formed you, and appointed you
> to be a light to all peoples,
> a beacon for the nations,
> to open eyes that are blind,

to bring captives out of prison,
out of dungeons where they lie in darkness.[6]

Through the exile and the prophecy of Second Isaiah, Israel came to embrace a broader view of reality, a deeper spirituality. They gained a consciousness that transcended a society that rejected Jews as misfits, a cosmic wisdom that comprehended the oneness of the universe in which Jews not only "belonged" but were essential instruments of God's plan of salvation. With this more inclusive view of reality, they were able to embrace the role of God's Suffering Servant. They became free enough to give and love—anyway.

It was no accident that both Jesus and his followers reached back to Second Isaiah to understand what they were being called to do. Jesus became the Suffering Servant personified. And he is there for gay Christians to claim as an exemplar.

When gay Christians can transcend society's too small concept of God and embrace, as Jesus did, the awesome and liberating reality that *all* of creation is redeemed, then it becomes possible for them to give and love anyway, as Jesus the Christ gave and loved in the face of a society that utterly rejected him.

We have now identified the gay predicament and have seen how important it is for gay Christians to develop a spiritual awareness that transcends society's too small view of God. We have established, then, a *goal* for therapy with gay people: deeper spiritual grounding. But how is that done in therapy? How can that goal be reached?

The next three chapters do not specifically pertain to gay patients. They explore the process of psychotherapy with an eye toward integrating the psychological and spiritual dimensions in the work. Then, in Chapter 8, we will return to the gay predicament and explore how the process specifically applies to gay people.

:5
The Pain, the Pain

I have never known anyone who has been in psychotherapy who didn't find it painful. Most people find it excruciating. Sheldon Kopp sardonically sums up the therapeutic torture chamber in these words: "The *bad* news about therapy . . . is that you *don't* die."[1]

My favorite metaphor for psychotherapy is orthodontistry. There are four parallels. They both cost a lot of money. They both take a long time. They both hurt, week after week. And (the good part), if you stick it out, you get to enjoy the benefits of either for the rest of your life.

One patient of mine simply calls my office "the rack."

The point is that, although most people end up believing it is worth it, psychotherapy hurts like hell.

Innovative therapies that attempt either to by-pass the pain or condense it keep appearing. Rational-emotive therapy, for instance, attempts to get around pain by thinking patients out of it.

> Primarily, RET (Rational-Emotive Therapy) employs a highly cognitive approach. It is based on the assumption that what we label our "emotional" reactions are mainly caused by our conscious and unconscious evaluations, interpretations, and philosophies.
>
> Like stoicism, a school of philosophy which originated some twenty-five hundred years ago, RET holds that there are virtually no legitimate reasons for people to make them-

selves terribly upset, hysterical, or emotionally disturbed, no matter what kind of psychological or verbal stimuli are impinging on them.[2]

I remember a RET psychologist telling me how he helped patients deal with being rejected in social settings. He logically explained to them that, if they approached someone and got a cold shoulder, they didn't need to feel rejected. What the person they had approached was rejecting was not *them* at all, but the constellation of projections he or she brought to the encounter and laid on them. Since those projections had nothing to do with the patients themselves, feeling rejected was simply unnecessary. Somehow, his total lack of sensitivity to a patient's normal hurt responses to being rejected left me cold.

Another example of a modern therapeutic attempt to bypass pain is behavior therapy. Behaviorism simplifies the business of pain by denying that feelings are anything more than a conglomeration of conditioned physical responses.[3] Rather than wasting psychic energy on feelings (which behaviorists dismiss as illusions), behavior therapists encourage patients to channel that energy into adopting behavior that avoids stressful situations.

Examples of therapies that try to condense the pain are *primal scream* (Janov[4]) or just plain *scream* (Casriel[5]) as well as some of the pop psychology experiences like est and Lifespring. All of these cathartic therapies seem to rely on one basic technique: putting patients in emotional pressure cookers. If all goes well, the patients burst, spewing forth all of their repressed anger and frustration. The theory is that, having gotten rid of all their pent-up rage and hurt emotively, patients are then free to move on.

The problem with either of these types of therapy—rational or cathartic—is that they don't work—at least for long. Est graduates, for instance, frequently fly around on an incredible high for several months after the experience, but then it wears off.

Rational-emotive graduates, on the other hand, seem to learn how to keep a stoic even keel most of the time, but when faced with a life crisis of major proportions, their ability to talk themselves out of feelings falls apart.

A colleague of mine named Michael is a rational-emotive therapist. Michael was a Spartan; it seemed that nothing could upset him. Downturns in his practice, problems with his adolescent son, staff dissension at the clinic where he practiced—all these difficulties he met with a logic so unshakeable that it made Mr. Spock from the "Star Trek" television series look like an hysteric.

Until his wife left him after fifteen years of marriage. He did his best to bear up. He spent hours with me, rationally contending that, while this might be difficult, there was no reason for him to be upset. She was not rejecting him; she simply felt the need to move on. Since it was nothing personal, he didn't need to take it personally. On and on he would go, peeling off logical argument after logical argument, trying to convince me that he didn't feel bad.

Late one evening, after listening to two hours of Michael's ratiocinations and watching him get wearier and wearier, I intervened. "Michael," I said, "the woman you've shared your life with for fifteen years, the woman who knows you better than anybody in the whole world, the woman you've cared for with all your heart and soul, made love to, and borne children with—she's *leaving* you—*forever*. It must be dreadful for you." Michael's eyes welled up; he tried to choke back the tears. As he sat there sputtering, I said gently, "Why don't you let yourself go, man? I promise I won't tell." And then he wept.

All I had done, of course, was hold a mirror up for Michael to see himself as he really was. The mirroring function is a large chunk of doing psychotherapy. Inviting people to look at themselves as they are—really are—as opposed to how they think they are. You see, Michael actually believed he was a Spartan. I happened to know that even Spartans were men, that no man is really any stronger than any other, and that all men bleed. All I had done was to give him permission to be weak, which was simply his inalienable right as a human being.

Besides not lasting long, rational and cathartic therapies don't turn out very well-rounded people. Rational-emotive and behaviorist graduates end up being very much in control of their lives, but not very much in touch with *life*. They seem, too often, to be automatons, responding appropriately, coping nicely, but living soullessly. Like victims of psychosurgery, they seem cut off from their frontal lobes. My friend Michael was a prime example. (He's different now.)

Cathartic graduates often appear to have substituted megalomania for low self-esteem. They do seem to be intimately in touch with every one of their feelings (at least superficial ones) but this self-awareness is usually coupled with such steely willfulness and unrelenting need for immediate gratification that the result looks like cultivated narcissism.

This past year a patient was referred to me by a neighborhood clinic. As I later found out (and initially suspected), the man was a Lifespring devotee. He left a message on my machine. When I returned his call and identified myself, without further ado, this is what he fired at me: "The clinic referred me to you for therapy. I can see you on Wednesdays at three. We'll start tomorrow."

As it happened, the only hour I had free at the time was at nine-thirty on Monday mornings. So I responded, "I can see you on Monday mornings at nine-thirty." "Nine-thirty A.M.?" he retorted. "On Monday morning?" "Right," I replied. "Nine-thirty on Monday morning is *very* inconvenient for me," he went on. "I *could* make it but don't you have any other time available?" "No," I replied. "At the moment, that's the only hour I have free." "In the whole week?" he snarled suspiciously. "I'd be glad to refer you to someone else," I replied. "I really can't believe you don't have even one hour someplace else where you could fit me in," he stated firmly. "You don't have to take the referral," I replied. There followed a long silence. Then he said, "O.K. I'll see you on Monday at nine-thirty."

In this case, my task was clear: to take good care of myself. I do twenty hours of therapy a week. The rest of my workday is for professional reading, writing, and ruminating, and for note taking about patients. I might have allowed my non-clinical time to be invaded by capitulating to this fellow's demand. But it was clear from the first interchange that this man would need to come to grips with his desperate need for control. Had I capitulated, he would have thought he had won. Regaining control of the therapy (which, after all, is my *job*) would have been an uphill battle thereafter. My unwillingness to be manipulated was simply a matter of adhering to the old Arab epithet, "Never let the camel get his nose in the tent."

The petulance, narcissism, and willfulness were, of course, patterns of behavior that had been established long before Lifespring. But this ego-building program had managed to lock those traits in so tightly for this fellow that it made the therapeutic journey all the harder.

Like the young man above, people who undergo cathartic therapies often become so channeled into an egosyntonic self-attentiveness that there is no longer any awareness of context—their own or anyone else's.

What both rational and cathartic therapies lack is integration. C. G. Jung put his finger on the defect in this epithet: "If you get rid of the pain before you have answered its questions, you get rid of the self along with it."[6] What Jung was cautioning us to always keep in mind is that therapy is both an affective and a cognitive process. Both thoughts and feelings must be explored and, what is more important, they must be tied together. Rational therapies capitalize on the cognitive, feelings are repressed, and something of the self is lost. Cathartic therapies get at the feelings, all right, but insufficient time is spent "answering the pain's questions." The cognitive is short-changed and, again, something of the self is sacrificed.

There are no shortcuts. It would be nice if there were, but there aren't. Therapy done well and done fully takes a long time. And what seems to take most of the time is the integrative process of moving from insight to insight at a slow enough pace and in an intentional enough way that thoughts and feelings get attached to each other. So the pain must be endured over a longer period of time? That's how it is. There are no shortcuts.

In sum, psychotherapy is a long and painful journey. Patients must, on their own steam, walk through the dark valley and explore it. You cannot just acknowledge that the darkness is there and then take a detour. Nor can you take a running leap and sprint through the sticky mess. You must walk slowly and deliberately through the terrifying labyrinthine recesses of your soul and explore them like an archaeologist looking for a shard in order to get to where you want to go.

And, of course, this is as true for the therapist as it is for the patient. Healers of souls who expect quick, miraculous cures, bereft of pain—their *own* pain—should be prepared for disappointment. Besides the arduousness and sorrow of being close companions on patients' painful journeys, healers expose themselves to the perils of enduring, intimate relationships that constantly confront them with their own fragilities. Therapy is no picnic, either for the therapist or the patient.

:6
Psychotherapy as Grieving

A nyone whose spouse has died can tell you about how hard grieving is and how long it takes. My seventy-one-year-old friend, Rachel, whose husband died last year, put it this way.

> It seemed like it would never end. I played it all back in my head, over and over again. I swear to God I remembered *everything* we ever did together. All the good things, and all the bad times, too. I'd remember something, and I'd cry. Cry because it was so beautiful or cry because it was so awful. I'd wait for him to come home, catch myself at it, and cry. I'd put two plates on the table for supper without thinking and I'd cry. I'd go to bed, want him there so bad, and I'd cry some more. For a while, I wanted to die too. You know, crawl right into the coffin with him. I thought it would never end.

> But it did. Little by little, I cried myself dry. And now? Hell, now I'm glad to be alive. And I'm out there getting all I can get!

You play it back over and over. You link feelings to recollections of experiences. You drink the pain to the dregs. You cry yourself dry. And then, somehow, the world brightens up again and you move on. That's what grieving is like.

Elizabeth Kubler-Ross[1] came up with a more scientific version of the grieving process based on her work with dying people. It has five steps: denial, bargaining, anger, depression, and acceptance. People who are dying seem to go through them in that order, although how fast they travel varies. Some people pass through all five stages in an instant. Some get stuck in one or several of them. Some never make it to acceptance at all. Like most models, no one ever fits exactly. It's a useful schema to understand something about therapy. Just don't take it too literally.

A friend of mine, dying of cancer, did the Kubler-Ross sequence almost perfectly. (When she got to the acceptance stage, I told her how proud she should be of herself for doing it right.) Her name was Ruth.

Ruth was a woman in her fifties. She had raised five children; one was still at home. He was fourteen. Her husband worked for the post office; she herself had worked for the local college as an administrative secretary.

Ruth was a tough lady: Teutonic, Lutheran, stubborn, matronly, hair pulled back in a French twist, heavy but solid, and buxom. She characterized herself as "a boy's mother." (Her one daughter wholeheartedly agreed.) That self-image usually got linked with one of her more common pronouncements, "I don't take any crap off anybody!" And believe me, she didn't. I don't think I ever saw her cry. Well, maybe once, but I wasn't sure.

A lump on Ruth's neck had been misdiagnosed as a benign fibroid tumor. A year later—too late, as it turns out—a biopsy revealed that it was a cancerous lymph node. Further tests showed that cancer had spread throughout her body, including her internal organs.

The doctor was honest with her. He said they would try chemotherapy and radiation, but thought the best they could do was slow it down. He gave her a year.

Ruth's first reaction was to call him and the whole hospital staff liars. (Ruth, you'll remember, didn't take any crap off anybody.) They had blown it a year ago. Why should she trust them now? They were all quacks.

She went to another physician. Then another. It took four confirmations before she believed it. And even then, all she would believe was that she had cancer. As far as Ruth was concerned, the dying part was still up for grabs.

Next she set about trying to get cured. She stopped smoking. She went on a diet. She started taking massive doses of vitamins. She went back to attending church regularly. And she underwent both radiation and chemical therapy, convinced (regardless of what *they* said) that the treatments could cure her. The cancer went into remission for a while, but then began spreading again.

But Ruth was stubborn. She badgered her husband into taking her to Mexico where she went to a Laetrile clinic for treatment. A month later, the cancer was worse; she had lost fifty pounds.

Finally, in a last desperate attempt to bargain, Ruth went to a faith healer, Kathryn Kuhlman.[2] She attended service after service, hoping that she would be one of the people Mrs. Kuhlman would announce had been cured. It never happened. Failing rapidly, Ruth ended up back in the hospital.

When I walked into the room the day after her readmission, the glare in her eyes made me want to run. I knew there was a powder keg lying in the bed; the last thing I wanted to do was light the fuse. So, naturally, I said the wrong thing. (Could I have said the right thing?) "How are you?" I asked stupidly. "Dying, idiot," she replied warmly. "How the hell am I supposed to feel? Happy?" Without further provocation, there followed ten uninterrupted minutes of railing at dumb doctors, quack Laetrile clinics, and heartless children. It wasn't fair. Nobody understood. Her grandmother had lived to be ninety. Her mother lived to be eighty. Why should she die at fifty? She wished we'd all leave her the hell alone! Then back to the stony silence.

I didn't stay long that visit. And, in fact, chicken that I was, I steered clear for a whole week. When I went to see Ruth again, she was a pitiful sight to behold. She had lost more weight. Her hair was a mess. All the bluster was gone. She lay slumped down in the bed, staring forlornly out the window at nothing. Broken. "Hi!" I said. "Hi," she sighed.

Her depression lasted a long time. We talked a lot during those weeks. And Ruth cried a lot. From here, the story sounds a lot like my friend Rachel's. She played tapes and cried, remembered and cried, dreamed of her husband's next birthday and cried. And eventually, she cried herself out.

The Ruth who emerged from the depression was different from the Ruth I had known. Most of the rigidity was gone. She didn't bluster so. She was gentler now. I rather liked her better this way.

As she came out of her depression, she set about doing what dying people have to do. She wrote goodbye letters to distant relatives. She updated her will. She finished up some needlepoint she had been stabbing at for years. She even planned her whole funeral service. And she philosophized. My, did she philosophize. She needed to pass on to us "kids" the very real wisdom she had gained.

Ruth refused painkillers to the end. It was the last remnant of her stubbornness. (You'll remember, Ruth didn't take any crap off anybody.) She died bright-eyed and bushy-tailed, physically a shadow of what she had been, but spiritually a giant.

Denial, bargaining, anger, depression, and acceptance: Kubler-Ross's five steps about how people deal with their own death. And Ruth did 'em all—by the numbers.

Kubler-Ross soon came to see that her model had broader application. The bereaved seem to grieve the same way the dying person does. Married people who are separating grieve, too. Grieving seems to be part and parcel of any major life event involving a loss.

But what about minor life events? Could it be that grieving is a regular, everyday activity of life that pertains to the most trivial as well as the most significant losses of our lives? Here is an example of how it might work at the trivial end of the scale.

One evening this past year, I went to see a film I had been looking forward to for a month. I arrived at the theater to find a line of expectant patrons extending clear around the block. After standing in line for forty-five minutes in the cold, the film sold out (about forty people before me). Worse still, I had put off going long enough so that this was the last night of the run, and the last show that evening. I wasn't going to get to see the film at all. There was nothing to do but grieve, and I can trace my journey through all five of Kubler-Ross's steps: denial ("They wouldn't let us stand out here in the cold if there wasn't room in the theater."); bargaining ("Maybe I'll be the last one to get in."); anger ("Damn it! I've waited a month to see this movie!"); depression ("Now I'll never get to see it."); and finally, acceptance ("Oh, well, there are other films to see. Maybe I'll catch this one on a rerun.").

The fact is that grieving is something we get the chance to do all the time. It is a process that can take place around any of life's disappointments, from not being able to turn left at an intersection marked "No Left Turn" to having to work a holiday, to losing a job, to losing a spouse, to dying.

Life is chock-full of disappointments and frustrations. As Sheldon Kopp would have it, "Life just keeps coming at you. The next problem is already on the way to you in the mail."[3] You would think, then, that people would develop grieving as a basic human skill. But in fact we don't. Many of us don't know how to grieve at all. Why?

In Chapter 2, we spent some time looking at "the myth." And, if you'll recall, there are some basic tenets of the myth, some truths held to be self-evident. First is that we are in control. What this boils down to is believing that, if we only do it right, we can always get what we want. Refusal to believe that we are ever helpless is a prerequisite for getting into the club.

There are other dogmas in the mythic credo as well, like: I am the center of the universe; I will be happy if I am good; life is rational and reasonable; evil is punished; God is in his heaven and all is right with the world; and so on. Buying into the myth demands that we put on blinders. We aren't allowed to look at reality, that life is a mixed bag over which we have little or no control and that the universe is a very indifferent place in which to live. Justice does not always triumph and evil is not always punished. Life is seldom fair and even less frequently rational.[4]

Approaching life through the myth automatically makes any and all disappointments warts on the nose of life's complexion. They don't fit. They conflict with the basic tenets of the myth's ideology.

There's only one logical thing to do about it: ignore them. Repress them. Deny them. Do whatever is necessary to make them go away. Warts are ugly; either have them removed or cover them over with makeup.

Another way of saying this is that we are culturally conditioned to repress all of the emotions associated with grieving. Panic, anxiety, anger, fear, depression—even acceptance (which mythmakers label *passivity*) are all considered anathema. "Don't panic! We'll find a way out of this." "You know, anxiety is just going to cause you high blood pressure. Take a valium." "Flying off the handle doesn't *solve* anything." "I'm getting awfully tired of you moping around like this." "Come on! Look at the bright side." "You have nothing to fear but fear itself." "Are you going to take this lying down?" Feelings of weakness are abominations in a society that needs to be in control.

The upshot is that most people don't learn to grieve well, if at all. Frequently, either through an accumulation of ungrieved life events or in the face of a major life tragedy that they have absolutely no skill to grieve about, people fall apart. We call such events "nervous breakdowns" or "psychotic breaks." We diagnose people who experience these events as having this or that condition to be cured. But what is wrong most often is that people who have breakdowns have often unwittingly hoarded their grief. Never having been taught how to grieve, they have simply accumulated pain and frustration for all of their lives.

Psychotherapy done well is a process through which patients learn how to grieve and begin grieving the storehouse of material they needed to grieve about all along but didn't.

The learning takes place mostly through the doing. The journey is made harder because it runs counter to the grain of everything the patient has been conditioned to believe. Helping patients get to the point of even *experiencing* the feelings associated with grief is an arduous, uphill climb. Helping patients explore old material that is painful and deeply buried is just as difficult. Tying the feelings to the thoughts is yet another time consumer.

Patients resist the process every inch of the way, usually. In psychoanalytic terms, this is called *resistance*. But it is not just contrariness, it is a mobilizing of the entire psychic apparatus to avoid doing what has been labeled and reinforced as unnatural and destructive. Giving in to grieving is to admit our weakness. It is a mythic taboo.

Integrative, spiritually oriented psychotherapy requires patients to learn to give up their egos' control over all that they do, think, and feel. For most patients, it means adopting a completely different way of living: taking life as it comes, embracing the pain that life includes, grieving those things that they want and cannot have as they present themselves, and moving on.

The range of things to be grieved about in therapy is mind-boggling, from the ridiculous to the sublime. Not only that, but grievables come firmly packed in layers. What are presented as *the* problems during the initial phase of therapy almost invariably end up being nothing more than the uppermost layer of a very high layer cake. Being stuck about what profession to choose, once lifted off and the icing scraped away, inevitably reveals some more basic internal conflicts.

A patient named Mark came to see me because, at twenty-six, he was still conflicted about what career to choose. On the one hand, he might want to go to medical school. His father was a physician. His grandfather had been a physician. He himself had majored in premed in undergraduate school. He had the brains. He even had some interest. What's more, he had been accepted into Harvard Medical School.

On the other hand, Mark thought he might like to be a painter. He had some talent, had sketched and painted as an avocation from high school on, had minored in art during his undergraduate years, and found it very fulfilling. A conundrum. What should he do?

Having graduated from college, Mark had bounced around for four years from one dead-end administrative job to another while he wrestled with this dilemma. He had even thought of solving the problem by becoming a commercial artist and drawing anatomical illustrations for medical trade journals. He just couldn't get unstuck, and coming to see me was a last resort to try to make up his mind.

It didn't take long to lift the layers off Mark's cake. Under the career dilemma itself lay the whole issue of parental expectations for his career versus his own desires. Why had he majored in premed? "I don't know. I guess I just always knew I would." Did he like it? "Oh, it was all right." The family tradition of the eldest son taking the Hippocratic oath was something Mark had taken for granted. There had been no direct pressure for his majoring in premed. He just did it because it was the thing to do.

Next layer down was the whole issue of "being his own man," the perennial problem of separating from parents. Attached to it were all the resentments he harbored about doing things their way ("Why should I go to medical school just to make them happy?") versus his need for their approval ("I think it will really break them up if I don't go into medicine."). Finally, underneath all of that was the constellation of unresolved stuff about what it had been like to be his parents' son. His father's formality and distance; his mother's preoccupation with "how things looked" to her family and friends.

> She didn't give a damn about what made *me* happy. It was always, "How would it look if . . ." or "What will the family think?" And my father? He's a stuffy old coot and always was. All he ever did was work. He was either at the hospital or his office or consulting or at a conference. Why would I

want to be like him? If that's what it means to be a doctor,
I'll clean streets!

Until Mark could sift through all the layers of pain, resentment, anger, and anguish he had built up toward his parents, there was no way for him to know what he really wanted
or needed or aspired to. He couldn't choose because there
were so many strings attached, either way.

Marital problems, adolescent problems, job problems—it
doesn't much matter what is presented at the outset. You can
always expect a layer cake.

The therapist's job is to help unpack that layer cake. It is
a process of helping patients identify what it is that they are
tenaciously clinging to and refusing to grieve, then helping
them, frequently in spite of themselves, to let go of the ties
that bind.

As you might expect, this is no simple endeavor. First of all,
patients are, most often, clinging to many attachments at the
same time. For Mark, some of these included his attachment
to being a dutiful son (as well as to being a rebellious one),
to having notoriety, to resentment against a father who had
never had time for him, to anger and disappointment toward
a mother whose only interest in him seemed to be as an ex-
tension of herself, and on and on.

It would have been nice if we could have dealt with each
grievable one at a time. But as is always true in therapy,
everything moves along in one messy piece. Rather like bread
dough. You knead it. You work flour into it. You pound on it.
You massage it. And eventually it becomes pliant and unified
and whole. But for most of the journey toward rising, bread
dough is a sticky, unwieldy mess.

In the course of one session, you might deal with a patient
whose fury at you would mean interpreting to feelings that
seemed related to his father. Fifteen minutes later, you might
be weeping with him about how unloved he had felt by his
mother. Another turn of the second hand and you might be
accompanying him on a fantasy shopping trip of possible
careers.

The therapist's job is to track patients where they are, walking alongside, sometimes being a neutral companion, sometimes a trickster, sometimes a lover, and sometimes "the enemy." Helping patients grieve at all the levels of the layer cake and through all the stages of grief is our job. Discerning what is going on at any given moment is challenging in itself. Responding in a way that gives people what they need at that moment is even more tricky. The techniques that are most useful at each stage of grieving are different, and timing is critical. The whole endeavor is challenging, nerve-racking, inexact, and fraught with perils. It often resembles a fast-moving board game. You frequently do the wrong thing. Perhaps eighty percent of a therapist's time is spent correcting previous errors. But helping patients through the grieving mill is the work.

Some of what patients need to grieve about is very old; in fact, much of it is. Destructive or damaging events from infancy, childhood, and adolescence that were buried and "forgotten" are the most common. If patients discover, for instance, that they are manipulative, chances are they will find the roots of that behavior in how they were treated as children. To the extent that they can go back, reclaim all of the outrage and hurt they buried along the way, look at the key experiences in which they were manipulated, and let go of that whole constellation of events, their behavior can change. They will no longer need to be manipulative. Having gone back and understood what those events meant to them (cognitive), having gone back and raged and wept over them (affective), and having linked the two together, they will no longer need to live out their revenge in their present life. Old material is a hefty layer of the therapeutic cake.

But not all of the material to be grieved about is historical. A good deal of it may be future-oriented. As an example, let's look again at Mark, who had thought that he might want to be a painter.

During periods when Mark was down on medicine, he would dream of being a great painter. He spent hours in art galleries, studied art history, and collected prints. He had developed an elaborate fantasy about what it would be like someday when he was a famous artist.

Somewhere along the line, Mark decided to take the plunge. He was ready. He had worked through enough of his layer cake to know for sure he didn't want to be a doctor. So it was time to try painting seriously. He enrolled in a graduate school of fine arts.

Not only did Mark do miserably at painting (by his own estimation although amply confirmed by his teachers), but he hated it. What he had enjoyed as an avocation he found boring and tedious as a profession. After six months, he began to loathe the sight of palette and canvas.

What Mark had to give up at that point wasn't something from the past, but something from the future: a cherished dream. It was a hard giving-up. Unrealistic expectations and cherished dreams are also common fare on the therapeutic grieving menu.

By the way, having rejected medicine and debunked painting, Mark got very confused. "Now what?" he said, feeling more stuck than he had before. He flailed around a good deal and, a year later, entered law school. He is now a patent attorney. Loves it.

Besides past and future grievables, there is a lot of current material that patients have to grieve about, too. Once they have gotten free of old stifling material and given up unrealistic expectations for the future, patients often take on whole new modes of being-in-the-world. They aren't the same people they used to be. They have different wants and needs, likes and dislikes. New options appear; creative energy is unleashed; clarity is gained.

In the course of therapy, people come to see bad marriages for what they are and decide to end them. They change career paths or give them up entirely. They cast aside everyday activities that no longer seem to work or nourish. They leave churches, or join them, or change denominations. They distance themselves from families, sever relations entirely, or reunite with them.

With a little luck, most of these major changes take place after therapy. If analytic theory is correct, major changes during the work can be dangerous externalizations of the internal therapeutic turmoil. But patients don't always wait. Sometimes they make decisions they later regret. It's all grist for the grieving mill.

Perhaps the hardest part of the present for patients to give up is the way they operate in the world—the ground rules they use in relating to other people. Psychologists call this process *breaking through characterological defenses.*

Just because patients come to understand the relationships between unresolved material from the past, present, or future, and how they behave now in the world, and even if good grief work is done around these harbored hurts, *changing* how they behave in the world does not happen automatically. The behavior, more likely than not, has developed a life of its own. It has been the means by which patients have coped for many years. It may not offer happiness, but it does offer security. It's familiar; it's what has worked.

A patient named Rob comes to mind. Rob had had one of the most controlling, manipulative, clutchy mothers you can imagine. She made "Momma" from the comic strip look permissive. No detail of Rob's life had escaped her domination: how he dressed, who his friends were, when he studied, where he studied, how he folded his socks, how his drawers were organized. She had not only controlled (through a joint account) the money he made working at odd jobs after school, she had made him account for every dime he spent. She had waited to make sure he got in on time every—no exceptions— *every* date and then had checked his neck for hickeys.

Rob came to therapy at age twenty-four because his lover, Glenn, threatened to leave him if he didn't. During an early session when I had asked Rob to bring Glenn along, we spent most of the hour hearing from Glenn about what a controlling, stifling, and manipulative bastard Rob was. Rob's response, of course, was to admit the behavior but justify all of it with air-tight rationalizations and moralisms. "Well, you *are* a slob. If I didn't get after you, you'd *never* clean the bath-room." Or, "You said you would be home at nine. Of course I was pissed at nine-fifteen! I was worried about you. You might have called."

During the course of the next year, Rob came to see—much to his chagrin—how much he was like his mother. He also did a solid job of grieving all of those years under her thumb. Murderous rage at how she had almost done him in, anguish for how little she had really loved *him*, as he was, who he was.

Still, he was—more or less—every bit as overbearing, con-trolling, and manipulative with his lover at the end of the year as he had been at the beginning. He would say things like, "I know what I'm doing. I know why I'm doing it. I don't want to do it. *But I can't stop!* He comes in ten minutes late and I go into automatic pilot!"

It took practice for Rob to give up his destructive ways of dealing with people. A lot of it got worked out in the thera-peutic transference.

Which is to say that Rob treated me no differently than anyone else in his life. His attempts to control me and the therapy were frequent, often sneaky, and dogged. I was sub-ject to the same passive aggression and self-righteousness he meted out to everyone else who was significant to him.

For example, one time I lost track of the hour with a pre-vious patient and began Rob's session five minutes late.

As always, I said nothing at the beginning of an hour. I simply waited and listened.

"Running a little bit behind schedule?" he asked coyly, looking into space.

I knew it was a set-up, but decided that the best way to respond was to bite. "Yes. I am late," I responded.

"That's not like you," he went on, with a subtle but dis-tinctly judgmental edge on his voice.

So it was to be one of Rob's favorite routines, "victim-vic-timizer." I made a connection with how he treated his lover when *he* was late and decided to fan the flames a little. "Yes," I replied. "And what's more, I was with another man."

"What's *that* supposed to mean?" he snorted self-righteously, glaring at me.

"I hear how pleased you are to have some grievance to hold over my head," I said.

"You *were* late," he retorted, pointing at the clock.

"Got me." I countered blandly.

The volleys continued for a while, during which I gave him lots of rein to hate my guts and let the negative transference develop fully. At some point, I made the interpretation, "You've just demonstrated how inviting it is for you to be a victim, and how much payoff there is in that for you. That's instructive." His countenance fell. The ensuing silence, as he slumped in his chair, let me know that I had "made a hit." He looked forlorn.

I changed gears. "Feeling exposed, huh?" I asked gently.

"Naked," he muttered.

"It's hard to look at the games."

"I do this all the time, don't I?" he asked.

"Probably," I answered.

Then we just sat.

Eventually, of course, once the meaning of my lateness to him and his reaction to it had been explored thoroughly, I apologized for my lateness and offered to make the time up at the end of the hour. To have done that at the outset, however, would have eclipsed the important opportunity for growth that in fact took place.

It would be a nice fantasy to imagine that Rob's behavior changed based solely on the insight from this one encounter. When I first began doing the work, I was naive enough and had grandiose enough notions to imagine that that would be true. As it was, Rob and I played out the same script, with a variety of contents, thirty or forty times before his destructive behavior in this area truly began to yield. But yield it did.

Towards the end of the therapy, Glenn lost his job. It was nothing new. (Glenn had his own stuckness to deal with.) He had lost three jobs in the past year. He was a waiter, would oversleep, be late, get suspended, and eventually fired. Each time, Rob would badger him mercilessly until he found another position. This time he decided he would keep his mouth shut. It almost killed him. He'd seen Glenn lying in front of the TV at eleven in the morning instead of being out pounding the pavement and he'd boil. He took to spending a lot of time in the bathroom. He dubbed it "the boiler room."

Much to his surprise (and disappointment) Glenn found a job all by himself in four days. "Isn't that amazing," I said glibly, "and all without the benefit of your badgering." Rob sneered (he had gotten to the point of being able to laugh at himself) and retorted haughtily, "He undoubtedly would have found a *better* job if I had done my number." We both roared.

Grieving destructive or self-destructive behavior is no easy undertaking. It may, in fact, be the hardest part of the work.

I have shared the concept of grieving as a metaphor for psychotherapy with a number of psychologists, many of them quite traditional. They've almost all shook their heads in assent. "That's an interesting way to look at it," they've said. "It's a useful model. I'll keep that in mind." Frankly, I was surprised and just a little disappointed. I was attached to thinking that I was proposing something radical; I rather like the role of maverick. I looked forward to more of a fight.

One evening, I was having dinner with a colleague whose field of expertise is stress management. Since I began working on this book, I had bounced some of its ideas off a number of friends, so I shared the grieving concept with him. He loved it. We talked about its relationship to Kubler-Ross; we applied it to a number of cases in each of our practices; and we looked at how it fit into each of our own journeys. I was feeling really understood.

Then, I shifted the conversation slightly and began drawing some links between grieving and letting go, between psychological grieving and spiritual grieving. I started using phrases like, "grieving our illusion of being in control," and "letting go of our sense of being powerful." At first, my friend just got confused. He looked increasingly perplexed, listened, grunted occasionally, but obviously didn't understand.

As a last resort, I offered an example. "Probably the hardest thing to grieve or let go of," I said, "is believing that all of the stuff you didn't get while you were young—all the loving and caring—is gone forever, that there's no way to get it back." Well, that got to him. The expression on his face changed from perplexity to horror. It was as though I had told him I had a gun under the table and was going to kill him. Puffing himself up and arching his back, he snapped, "Well, that's where we part ways. I don't accept that. I don't believe it. I *can* make up for what I never got. I *can* get it." He was so upset that he refused to talk about it any more. Shortly thereafter, he made some excuse and left.

Then it was clear. The *process* of grieving seems palatable right across the board. But where the ego-bound therapist and someone on the spiritual path part ways is when the latter suggests that the ego—any piece of it or any of its power—is also grist for the grieving mill. Ego-centered therapy can make sense of grieving old, future, and current material, but only if the goal is to make *me* stronger.

This anecdote also points up another common therapeutic occurrence. My stress management friend resembled, in this instance, many patients who, when truly confronted with those pieces of themselves that keep them most stuck, out and out refuse to give them up. It may be said as "I can't," or "I don't know how," or more honestly as "I won't." But they all belie a firm resistance to changing. As a colleague of mine says, "Most people aren't afraid that therapy won't work; they're afraid that it will."

My stress management acquaintance still tries to live out his incomplete childhood script. He is gay, and, in what seems like an endless procession, gets involved with older men— father figures—whom, he says, never give him the love he wants. Perhaps someday he will figure out that no one can compensate him for the loving father he never had. Perhaps he won't. One thing is for sure, though: until he grasps that piece of reality and grieves his irretrievable loss, he is stuck.

In any case, this vignette is about the ego, in this case clinging tenaciously to a former, familiar, if destructive, map of the universe. And giving up any of ego's control is the dividing line between spiritual and nonspiritual approaches to therapy.

Some more will be said about this rift at the conclusion of

the next chapter. But something needed to be included here to avoid confusion. When I have spoken of therapy in this chapter, I have always meant integrative, spiritually grounded therapy. It is not therapy based on the Freudian epithet: "Where the id was, there ego shall be," but on a post-Freudian epithet that might go: "Where ego was, there 'just being' shall be." A Christian might say it: "Where ego was, there God shall be."

So what does all this therapeutic grieving get you? You subject yourself to two or more years of grueling exploration of the darkest recesses of your being, strip yourself naked before the universe, spend many a week in a fog, and toss many a night wrapt in tumultuous dreams. There had better be something good at the end of the rainbow, right? Well, there's bad news and good news here, too.

The bad news is that you do not live happily ever after; you do not end up with permission to be a "bliss-ninny" for the rest of your days. Life continues to be a mixed bag of joy and sorrow, pleasure and pain, and you are guaranteed to get some of each. Nor does life intrinsically get any less convoluted or complex. You will still find yourself in situations that boggle the mind.

The good news is that, if you have worked hard and grieved well and learned how and when it is appropriate to grieve, you will have given up attachments to much that is not and never was real. You will have cut yourself free of fetters that have bound you hand and foot.

Three words keep presenting themselves to me: freedom, equanimity, and peace. Unattached to a lot of material that has nothing to do with who you are (as opposed to who you were or might be or who you've thought yourself to be), you will be better able to just *be here now*,[5] unselfconsciously doing whatever it is that you do. Some of it will be hard and painful, but you will face it and do what you need to do. Some of it will be ecstatically joyous, and you will be able—as perhaps never before—to drink that joy to the bottom of the glass. *Being here now* ultimately means being free of the tyranny of the ego, as well. Not just freedom from everything *out there*—past, present, and future—but freedom from everything *in here*, too—freedom from our *selves*.

Equanimity refers to a whole attitude toward the world. It assumes no need to control or make life happen. It is not passivity, but an active participation in whatever is happening. It is doing whatever is natural to do, which may mean screaming or weeping, laughing or just sitting and watching. Equanimity assumes nothing about what is going to happen, imposes no dogma on what should happen. It simply allows life to unfold as it unfolds, including whatever it is that I will do in whatever situations that arise.

Peace is perhaps the bottom line, and I hesitate to even use the word. Unlike freedom and equanimity, peace cannot be a goal. It is more like a by-product. Peace here does not mean sylvan and bucolic tranquility, a life free of turmoil and strife. It is mostly an internal experience of at-onement with the flow of the universe.[6] It is quite possible to experience profound inner peace in the midst of a most painful life event.

A disclaimer. I have not meant to claim here that, after therapy, people will have reached anything near the pinnacle of spiritual enlightenment. I somehow cannot give my ego sufficient rein (reign?) to achieve the hybris of some psychoanalysts who actually believe that patients can eventually be completely analyzed. Two or three years of therapy (or seven or eight years of analysis) does not guarantee attainment of *atma* or union with God.

I would hazard a guess, though, that most patients who have had successful therapies—therapies that attend to both psychological and spiritual dimensions—experience more freedom, equanimity, and peace than they ever have before. Good therapy helps patients do two things: get launched onto a path leading toward enlightenment and learn some navigational techniques and tools to expedite their journeys. The journey itself is life; therapy is no more than a major intervention along the way.

:7
Spiritual Growth as Grieving

In the last chapter, we looked at psychotherapy as a grieving process. We saw that grieving is a recurring, lifelong task, a part of living that involves giving up attachments to those things that are gone forever, unattainable, or never were. We characterized therapy as an experiential training course in grieving.

We got a taste of how grieving happens in the spiritual realm in the last chapter. But most of what we looked at—the ideas, the jargon, the anecdotes—came from a Western psychotherapeutic context. In this chapter, we will take a look at grieving from the perspective of the other strand of our double helix, the spiritual one.

To begin with, spiritual awakening is no less like orthodontistry than psychotherapy. Spiritual teachers have warned us for centuries that the journey is painful. Christians traditionally have been cautioned that a life of contemplation (somewhat arrogantly called *the life of perfection*) is not for everyone, that it is a special vocation to which few are called. Eastern teachers also do their best to discourage people from setting off on the path. Chogyam Trungpa quotes these ominous words: "Better not to begin. Once you begin, better to finish it."[1] He goes on to say, "Once we commit ourselves to the spiritual path, it is very painful and we are in for it. . . . It will be terrible, excruciating, but that is the way it is."[2]

In the spiritual realm, too, people are always looking for shortcuts in order to avoid the pain. Some think they'll get there quicker by working from the outside in. I happen to be intimately acquainted with this one; it's how I got started.

I related in Chapter 1 the way in which some spiritual seeds were planted in me during my Roman Catholic rearing. I also wrote about how it took twenty years to pry them loose from all of the weeds. Eventually, though, they were ready to sprout. But at thirty, who wants to start at the bottom?

I began by donning all of the appropriate trappings. I read Ram Dass. I learned how to sit in a lotus position (agonizing, but I was determined to "look" right). I learned some Yoga exercises. I took meditation classes. I tried eating a vegetarian diet (unsuccessfully). And, having learned the spiritual jargon, I scattered it about liberally to enhance my image. Ultimately, I willed myself into a detached, tranquil state of peace. And it only took six months!

It looked about right, and a number of people got taken in. (Not my spouse, fortunately.) There was nothing malicious about it, of course. I really did think I was achieving spiritual enlightenment and I really did want it. But what I actually achieved was a colossal ego trip. There was so much self in-volved in the whole thing that I ended up more encumbered than I had been before I began. It took a while to figure that out. It's taken ever since to undo it.

Other people's motives for starting at the wrong end may be to avoid the more psychological sort of grieving. Petrified of their own murderous rage, they submerge it under a calm or "spiritual" exterior. They haven't "seen the light" at all, of course; they've only obliterated the darkness. If you look close, the serene smile often looks suspiciously like a reaction formation.

Others attempt instant spiritual arrival through drugs such as LSD. Richard Alpert (now Baba Ram Dass) began his spir-itual journey that way. He discovered it didn't work.

> For many of us who have come into meditation through psychedelics, the model we have had for changing con-sciousness has been of "getting high." Many of us spent long periods of time getting high and coming down. . . . My guru,

in speaking about psychedelics, said, "These medicines will
allow you to come and visit Christ, but you can only stay
two hours. . . . This is not true samadhi. It's better to become
Christ than to visit him." In view of his words, when I re-
flected on my trips with LSD and other psychedelics, I saw
that after a glimpse of the possibility of transcendence, I
continued tripping only to reassure myself that the possibility was still there. Seeing the possibility is indeed different from being the possibility. Sooner or later, you must
purify and alter your mind, heart, and body so that the
things which bring you down from your experiences lose
their power over you.[3]

As with psychotherapy, there don't appear to be any shortcuts on the spiritual journey. In Trungpa's words,

Understanding does not mean that you actually do it; you
just understand it. . . . The only way to get to the heart of
the matter is to actually experience it. . . . The problem is
that we tend to seek an easy and painless answer. But this
kind of solution does not apply to the spiritual path. . . .[4]

Again we are looking at a long and painful journey. And
again, the journey takes as long as it does because it requires
a lot of tearing apart, remembering, agonizing over, and letting go. If Ram Dass is right, and spiritual growth is a matter
of "purifying and altering our minds, hearts, and bodies," we
are committing ourselves to a major overhaul of who we are.
That doesn't happen overnight. Trungpa puts it this way to
those who are contemplating spiritual formation: "We have
committed ourselves to the pain of exposing ourselves, of taking off our clothes, our skin, our nerves, heart, brains, until
we are exposed to the universe. Nothing will be left."[5]

Kubler-Ross's five steps just as aptly describe the journey
of spiritual awakening as they do psychotherapy. Denial, bargaining, anger, depression, and acceptance are all familiar
milestones on the road to enlightenment.

In his book, *Cutting through Spiritual Materialism*, Trungpa
offers a story about a great Buddhist guru named Milarepa,
and how he came to give up his attachment to *wanting* en-

lightenment, perhaps the ultimate thing for someone on the spiritual journey to let go of.

[Milarepa] was a peasant . . . [who] had committed many crimes, including murder. He was miserably unhappy, yearned for enlightenment, and was willing to pay any fee that Marpa [his teacher] might ask. So Marpa had Milarepa pay on a very physical level. He had him build a series of houses for him, one after the other, and after each was completed, Marpa would tell Milarepa to tear the house down and put all of the stones back where he had found them, so as not to mar the landscape. Each time Marpa ordered Milarepa to dismantle a house, he would give some absurd excuse, such as having been drunk when he ordered the house built or never having ordered such a house at all. And each time Milarepa, full of longing for the teaching, would tear the house down and start again.

Finally, Marpa designed a tower with nine stories. Milarepa suffered terrific physical hardship in carrying the stones and building the house. When he had finished, he went to Marpa and once more asked for the teachings. But Marpa said to him, "You want to receive teachings from me, just like that, merely because you built this tower for me? Well, I'm afraid you will still have to give me a gift as an initiation fee."

By this time, Milarepa had no possessions left whatsoever, having spent all his time and labor building towers. But Damena, Marpa's wife, felt sorry for him and said, "These towers you have built are such a wonderful gesture of devotion and faith. Surely my husband won't mind if I give you some sacks of barley and a roll of cloth and offered them as his fee, along with the gifts of the other students. But Marpa, when he recognized the gifts, was furious and shouted at Milarepa, "These things belong to me, you hypocrite! You try to deceive me!" And he literally kicked Milarepa out of the initiation circle.

At this point, Milarepa gave up all hope of ever getting Marpa to give him the teachings. In despair, he decided to commit suicide and was just about to kill himself when Marpa came to him and told him that he was ready to receive the teaching.[6]

What Milarepa initially couldn't give up was believing that he could control, earn, or somehow through his own effort *take* the teachings from Marpa. So he began by denying his helplessness. All of the house building was bargaining—a quite literal kind of bargaining—while he tried to negotiate a proper payment to acquire the teachings. He progressed through frustration (buried anger) and, in deep depression, came to the point of suicide. At that moment, Marpa intervened with the necessary nudge to push Milarepa over the line into acceptance. (Gurus are like that.)

This example probably seems like grieving at a very esoteric level. It is. But those on the spiritual journey aren't called upon only to surrender things of great spiritual profundity; they usually begin much more basically. Giving up hot dogs is just as excruciating for a chela who enters a vegetarian ashram.

And, in fact, in the Eastern tradition at least (and increasingly in the West), since psychology and spirituality haven't been divorced from each other, the whole bag of grievables talked about in the last chapter is also grist for the spiritual mill. From not being able to turn left at a sign saying "No Left Turn" to the death of a spouse, from past pain and anguish to future cherished dreams, the whole gamut of material must be dredged up, mourned about, and given up on the way to spiritual enlightenment.

Spiritual growth like psychotherapy, then, is a process of grieving. You begin by practicing how to do it and then spend the rest of your life doing it. Those who attain enlightenment or union with God have done it, given up attachment to everything. They've even given up attachment to getting attached. Don't expect to meet many people like this in a lifetime.

But there is a major difference between grieving from a traditional psychotherapeutic vantage point and grieving from a spiritual point of view. I alluded to it toward the end of the last chapter. More needs to be said. The difference has to do with the ego.

In psychotherapy as envisioned in the West, the goal of therapeutic grieving is giving everything over to the ego. In spiritual formation, the ultimate goal is letting go of everything—*especially* the ego—giving everything over to God or cosmic consciousness or the cosmic flow.

It includes giving up attachment to all of the grievables mentioned so far. But it includes much more: desire for worldly goods, power, status, relationships; the need for affirmation by other people; the need to keep our egos reassured that we exist by constantly defining ourselves apart from the other; the need to define ourselves at all; the need for the dualistic thinking that gives rise to the I-Thou dichotomy; the need for the security that leads to such a dualistic world view. The spiritual goal is at-onement with the flow of the universe, which requires letting go of all that gives us comfort and a sense of self-determination. Everything we have used to reinforce our *selves* has to go.

As we saw in Chapter 2, this whole way of being flies in the face of what we are taught. We are again looking at a way of coming at the world that looks crazy to the mythmakers, who want to define reality as what we can control or fix. The need to not feel the helplessness of being human—of being ultimately powerless—forces us, through the ego, to define light as darkness and darkness as light. The spiritual dimension is called *illusory* and dismissed, and the fantasy world of our own making—a world of naming, conceptualizing, and controlling—is held up as real and concrete.

People seek spiritual direction because they are starving for more meaning in their lives. They have a sense that there must be something more but have no idea what it is. They come to a teacher or spiritual director at their wit's end of trying to *get* it, wanting to know what to *do* next.

All of the wanting and trying, of course, is the ego at work. Since the only way to achieve enlightenment is by giving up the ego, exercising it this way only makes it more impossible. What they don't know is that what they want may not be acquired by striving.

If they only just gave up the striving, they would have what they want instantly. But it never happens that way. In Trungpa's words:

> The experience of sunyata [openness] cannot be developed without first having worked through the narrow path of discipline and technique. Technique is necessary to start with, but it is also necessary at some stage for the technique to fall away. From the ultimate point of view the whole process of learning and practice is quite unnecessary. We could perceive the absence of ego at a single glance. But we would not accept such a simple truth. In other words, we have to learn in order to unlearn.[7]

You may have noticed that there is a paradox here. It gives rise to a lot of enjoyable reading in stories about gurus and their disciples. What Trungpa refers to as "learning and practice" is all rolled up with exercising the ego. It seems strange to exercise your ego if the ultimate goal is to give it up, but that's how it is. It's rather like spinning your wheels.

You're driving your car and you get stuck in the mud. You start to spin your wheels. You get frustrated. You even try rocking the car, but it won't budge. You get even more frustrated. So you start spinning your wheels faster and faster until they are almost buried in the mud. By now you are totally exasperated. And finally you give up.

And then a funny thing happens. Just at the moment when the wheels are about to go under, just when you've screwed your insides up into a gargantuan knot, just when your ego has reached its wit's end of trying to *make* it happen, when you throw up your hands and scream, "The hell with it!" that's when you get it! The wheels lift out of the rut and off you go down the road.

The paradox is that exercising the ego—in fact, pushing it to its limits—is seen as absolutely essential for spiritual growth, but only so you get to figure out how dumb it is.

Spiritual formation, then, is a process of learning how to surrender and begin giving up attachments to all of the things, ideas, feelings, and ways of being-in-the-world that keep us from just simply being, doing what is accurate and appropriate at the moment. Being here and now means being in the flow of the universe. Being here and now means participating in being, allowing ourselves to be fully a part of God's plan of salvation. To the extent that we are distracted from the moment by our attachment to whatever, we are out of the flow, out of synch with the unfolding universe.

True spiritual enlightenment means learning a whole new way of living for most of us. It means embracing a life of openness to what is as it occurs, a commitment to giving up attachment to things as they present themselves and that we inevitably become tied to. The ultimate hope is that the initial impulse to get attached in the first place will diminish as we spiritually mature.

What is the payoff for years of agonizing self-searching and surrender? What do disciples hope to achieve by the miseries they lay themselves open to at the hands of their gurus?

A common word used to describe the state aspired to is *transcendence*, "being in the world but not of it." That is to say, living in the moment—always in the moment—but not being attached to anything that presents itself in that moment. Freedom just to be and be fully, doing whatever it is that the moment requires, experiencing whatever it is that the moment holds, be it pain or pleasure, joy or sorrow, but existing and participating completely and authentically in that moment.

The experience of transcendence is peaceful. There is no demanding or coercing, no regrets or expectations, no analyzing: just being. All of the psychic energy that we normally waste in doing something other than being present is let flow, as it is intended, into the stream of life. It is an experience of effortlessness—not lethargy, because there is an overwhelming sense of energy flow—but effortlessness, in the sense that there is no bucking the flow of what is.

When you give in to the flow, it empowers you. It is the power of love, and so you become free to love. You become an instrument of love.

I wanted an example for the end of this chapter, a clear and
striking illustration of someone's spiritual journey to total
union with God. As it happens, I am writing on Palm Sunday,
the beginning of Holy Week. What more striking example of
the spiritual journey to total union with God than that of
Jesus of Nazareth?

Jesus knew what it meant to be attached to things: his
mother, zeal for his Father's house, contempt for the priests
and Pharisees. Perhaps more than anything else, he was attached to his ardent desire that people truly *hear* the good
news he came to share.

In three short years, he let go of all those attachments. But
not without racking pain. The temptation in the desert, throw-
ing the money changers out of the temple, trying in vain to
be understood, and finally agonizing in the garden. All pieces
of giving up to his Christhood, all parts of his letting go.

The Jesus who prayed, "Father, if thou art willing, remove
this cup from me," wanted to *live*. He knew he had to suffer.
He knew he had to die. It was a torturous fate to accept. He
sweated blood over it, we are told. At least until he got to the
words, "nevertheless, not my will, but thine be done."

By the time he got up from praying in Gethsemane, Jesus
had just about made it. His union with God was all but complete. Oh, there was some final hesitance: "I thirst." and "My
God, my God, why have you forsaken me?" But there was no
more bucking the flow. Jesus' silence during his trial and his
willingness to participate fully in all that he envisioned would
happen to him (and did) make that clear. So do the rest of his
words from the cross: "Father, forgive them . . . ," "Woman,
behold your son . . . ," "into Your hands . . . ," "It is finished."

It's hard to believe that Jesus was at peace as he hung there.
How could you be at peace with thorns sticking into your
head, your back slashed to ribbons, and spikes driven through
your wrists and feet? But I believe he was. Totally in the
moment. Not wanting it to be different from how it was. Not
yearning for it to be over. Just doing what had to be done.

And we call him the Christ. Why? Not because he is the
only person to have died for his faith. Lots of people have

done that. And not because he achieved union with God, either. Others have done that, too. We call him Christ because no one before or since has both loved so totally and given up so much. He came bearing all love, and allowed himself to be consumed by all evil. The odds he faced on the journey to enlightenment were overwhelming; only God could have done it.

In the end, how was it for him? There was no demanding or coercing. No regrets. No expectations. No analyzing. He was just being. Just simply being. Just simply being crucified.

:8
Grieving Gay

W e've looked at the journey. We've looked at the myth. We've looked at grieving. We've come to see that grieving is a useful metaphor for both psychotherapy and spiritual formation, but that there is a difference. Traditional psychotherapy aspires to give everything over to the ego. Spiritual formation aspires to give the ego up, too. Now we must look at how all of this relates to the gay predicament.

In the course of a lifetime, some people have to grieve more than others. There's no reason for it. It isn't necessarily fair. "Man asks, 'why me?' God answers, 'Why not' "[1] There is little use in calling it cruel and inhuman. It is just how it is.

There is a danger in even *saying* "Some people have to grieve more than others." It can trigger obnoxious outpourings of indulgent self-pity. After all, what do you get from knowing that you have a harder row to hoe than the next guy? When all's said and done, your row is your row.

But in order to understand why gay patients need more spiritual nourishment than most other people, it is important to know what makes their situation different. We saw earlier that gays are excluded from the myth, from the structures and systems that most people use to gain a sense (albeit false) of security and well-being. We took a look at what this means already. We saw a few examples of how it works. It is time to look it square in the eye. What is the experience of grieving gay?

People tend to underestimate the plight of gay people. Gays soft sell their lot mostly because they've gotten used to it; it feels "normal." Bleeding-heart heterosexuals understate gay oppression mostly to assuage their consciences. "Oh, it's not really so much worse for gays. Things are tough all around." And, of course, conservative reactionaries (Moral Majority types) think that anything short of burning at the stake is too lenient.

As a way to avoid such minimizing, let's take some time to peruse a sampler of the things most gay people have to give up. I don't intend this survey to be a manifesto, a declaration of grievances, or a prelude to "poor us." It is here for one purpose only: to make clear how it is.

Let's start with relationships. How about families? I haven't known too many openly gay people whose families welcomed them with open arms. Partial or utter rejection are more common reactions.

Since a friend of mine came out to his mother, he hasn't heard from her. It's been three years. He is the oldest of three children; she now talks about her two kids.

More common is partial rejection. "O.K. Now we know," parents of another friend of mine said to him when he told them he was gay. "But don't *ever* mention it to us again!" He still goes home for visits, but there's that awful hole there, that huge part of his being that he's not allowed to share with them: his lover, their life together—its pains, its joys.

Badgering and ridicule from those nearest and dearest are also common fare for gay people. The story of Tim from Norman Brown's book is a breath-taking example of that. But it's a fairly ordinary story. Like a patient whose alcoholic mother calls him twice a week and begins each conversation with lines like, "Well, who's my queer son screwing around with *this* week?"

Gay people who were heterosexually married and have children often face a very painful kind of grieving having to do with child custody and visitation rights. Recently in Virginia, a lesbian mother legally lost all right of contact with her son.

After divorcing her husband, she was given custody of the

child. She began living with a lesbian lover; her ex-husband remarried. One evening, he arranged to pick up their son purportedly to go to a dinner party. They never returned.

He took the child out of state, called his ex-wife, and told her he was keeping the boy. She was upset but they agreed she could visit.

Some months later, the man's new wife sued to adopt the child, basing her argument on the mother's unfitness because of her sexual preference. She won. The boy's mother is now forbidden to have any contact with her son at all.

Granted, this is a dramatic example. But most gay male and lesbian parents face tremendous grief and pain around the issues of child custody and visitation rights.

So much for families. Then there are relationships with friends. Gay people who come out after having lived secretively for a number of years usually hope to keep their straight friends. Sometimes they do. Most often, they don't. Sometimes they are just out and out cut off. "You're *what*?" If not cut off, they are seen as an embarrassment to socialize with or invite over. "I'd love to have you two over for my birthday party," a woman told a lesbian couple I know, "but it would freak my mother out. Maybe just the three of us could get together sometime." They never did.

Having a gay friend often touches a raw nerve in straight people. So many Americans have unresolved sexual conflicts that a gay person evokes in them a shadow side of themselves that they find terrifying. It's nothing personal, of course, but it makes them drift off anyway.

The fact is that when gay people come out, they usually end up in a ghetto.

What happens with co-workers is about the same story as what happens with friends, but it's more frightening. After all, unless you quit, you are "stuck" with your workmates. If an openly gay person encounters a homophobic co-worker or boss—even if they can't be fired—life at work turns into a perpetual hassle.

Being gay means giving up many personal relationships. But there's lots more to let go of. Take, for example, security.

First, there is job security. In most places in the United States, employers with impunity can fire gay employees "just because." It often happens. Take, for instance, my boss at the software firm. The company was located in Maryland where there are no protective laws for gay people. He *legally* could have fired me on the spot. (The only reason he didn't, by the way, was because he was afraid of publicity.)

In the few places where homosexuals *are* protected by law from discrimination in employment, there are still tried and true techniques for getting rid of gay employees. (They were perfected on blacks and women.) You either don't promote them, or harass them, or disenfranchise them. They eventually leave. Like my friend Judith.

Judith was assistant director of a college library in Washington, which *has* protective laws. A new male director was hired and soon discovered that Judith was lesbian. He found out by pestering her for a date until she finally told him she was homosexual and had a lover. Over the course of the next three months, he divested her of her entire job, giving pieces of it—a little here and a little there—to other employees. He even stopped inviting her (the assistant director, you'll remember) to staff meetings. Her days consisted of sitting at her desk reading library journals.

When salary increase time came around, unlike her one-time subordinates who got seven percent raises or more, Judith got nothing.

She stuck it out for nine months, hoping it would blow over. It didn't. And mind you, all the while, as he slowly "stuck it to her," the director was *most* cordial.

After nine months, Judith started looking for another job. She eventually found one. But the director still managed to get in a parting shot. He refused to give her a recommendation. In his words, "I just haven't been able to get a feel for what you can do."

Although I know of no studies that substantiate this, I suspect that the majority of openly gay people fall into the lowest national income categories.

But there are other things to be secured besides jobs. Like

your rights and your health and maybe even your life. Gay people who need legal or police protection generally don't get it. Refusal of a lease on an apartment because the resident manager "can't stand fags," dismissal from a job, or denial of credit are usually lost causes for gay people in terms of recourse.

Homosexuals who get beaten up by "queer-baiters" or "rolled" have learned not to bother dialing 911. Police attitudes in many places (especially rural ones) are commonly, "They got what they deserved." Worse, in a lot of cases, gay victims don't report such incidents because they're afraid of "blowing their cover."

A friend of mine, Ken, visited a man in Chicago last Christmas. Saturday night, they were walking through the city (just walking, mind you—not holding hands, embracing, or otherwise "flaunting" their gayness). A carload of young thugs pulled up, assumed that the two were gay, dragged Ken off to a van, beat him unconscious, and dumped him in a gutter thinking he was dead. Actually he only had a severe concussion, two black eyes, loose teeth, and bruises from one end of his body to the other.

Anyway, Ken went to the police. They sized him up, figured he was "one of them," took the report *pro forma*, and, as he left the station, told him amusedly that he shouldn't expect to hear from them.

Aside from giving up protection, there is living with outright legal persecution. In most states, homosexual acts are considered felonies. For example, were I and a lover to move to Virginia, we could successfully be prosecuted and imprisoned for making love. (Incidentally, in Virginia, we could also be refused driver's permits and drinks in a bar.)

An attempt by a gay person to make social contact with someone on a sidewalk can be dangerous. A gay man I knew walked up to a man he found attractive (in an area where gay people hang out) and, thinking he was gay, gave him "the eye" and pulled out a terribly tired old line, "Got a light?" What he got was arrested by a plainclothesman for "soliciting." (Could you imagine a straight man being arrested for "putting the make on" a woman in the same context?)

Being in a gay bar (unfortunately the only social outlet for many gay people) can reap harassment or arrest outside for "loitering" or "jaywalking" or arrest inside on equally trumped-up charges if the bar is raided. If gay people get jailed on manufactured charges like these, they can expect degrading treatment, not to mention being prime targets of sexual assault.

What about security in religious institutions? Surely, the bosom of Holy Mother Church. Well actually, more often than not, churches foment homophobia. Gays can expect to be excommunicated or excoriated by fundamentalists, evangelicals, Roman Catholics, Mormons, Baptists, and most Lutheran or Methodist congregations. Presbyterians, Episcopalians, the United Church of Christ, Unitarians, and Quakers (especially the last three) are more accepting of gays, but even there, acceptance means tolerance.

Ordination is denied gay people in all denominations except the United Church of Christ and the Unitarian Church. Marriage for gays is forbidden by all denominations, which at the same time condemn homosexuals for engaging in "promiscuous sex," i.e., sex outside of marriage.

Another whole set of exclusions from the myth are applied specifically against gay couples. Since gay marriages are denied legal recognition in every state of the union, the legal and financial benefits that accrue to straight married people are legally denied gay people. Take Penny.

Penny is an older woman, who lived with her lover Melissa for seventeen years. They owned a home together, all of its furnishings, a summer cottage, and a boat.

Melissa died last year. In her will, she specifically left everything to Penny. Melissa's family, who had had nothing to do with her for years, became greedy after she died. They contested the will on the grounds that Penny and Melissa were "unrelated" and that Melissa, by virtue of being homosexual, was "mentally unsound." In the rural county where the case

was tried, the family won. Penny, at fifty-eight, lost everything: the house, the cottage, the boat—even the bed she and
Melissa had slept in for seventeen years. Such wills are rou-
tinely broken, and many a gay spouse or lover has been left
broken and penniless.

Equally oppressive is that, just as gay people can't legally
marry, so they can't legally divorce. Since gay people who
separate can be just as vicious as straight people in the same
predicament, things can get pretty ugly. But all of the protections that civil law provides for separating straight couples
are missing in the case of gay couples.

Then there is a potpourri of subtle ways in which gay couples get passed over by the myth. Listing a gay spouse or lover
as beneficiary on a life insurance policy is usually impossible;
joint applications for auto insurance (even on a jointly owned
car) are denied; health insurance inclusion for a gay spouse
is disallowed; and filing joint income tax returns is prohibited.
Public displays of affection—a kiss goodbye to a lover on a
street corner, an arm-in-arm stroll, a spontaneous hug, danc-
ing—can in most places reap a gay couple anything from
arrest for "lewd and lascivious conduct" to sniggers and gig-
gles to being beaten to a pulp.

Next are the double-binding, no-win imponderable social
situations. What do you do when invited to a party that you
know is going to be suburban straight and the host says,
"Bring a friend"? If you leave your lover home, you both feel
awful; if you go together, you both feel awful uncomfortable.

And what do gay couples do about visiting relatives, especially around holidays? Let's say the couple isn't out. With
their families expecting them each home, either they go to
their respective homesteads (and miss the most important
days of the year together) or they spend the holidays together
(and deal with confusion and fury on the home front). If the
couple is out, the situation is usually no better. Families who
may tolerate having a gay son or lesbian daughter home for
Christmas most often forbid them to bring along a lover or
spouse. The same double-bind obtains.

Notice that the list so far is skewed toward adult gay people who are to some degree open about their sexuality. But what about homosexuals who are too afraid to come out?

We who live in cities often err by generalizing from our own urban experience where gays have more freedom and protection. But most people don't live in cities. Many live in rural areas where being openly gay is a terrifying prospect.

For three years, I lived with a lover in a rural county of Maryland. We spent a good deal of time locked in a very claustrophobic closet. There were both shades and drapes at all of our apartment windows and we made a furtive ritual of closing them whenever we came home.

I held a prominent position in the county government, and he taught in a parochial school. The schizophrenia of our lives was almost unbearable. I weighed fifty pounds more than I do now, developed alarmingly high blood pressure, underwent two G.I. series in a year to try to detect a suspected ulcer, carried medication around to treat regularly recurring stomach cramps, and suffered from insomnia and severe headaches. And I was only twenty-six!

It was "red-neck" country. Besides tobacco farming and shellfish harvesting, the major county occupation was drinking. It wasn't a crazy paranoid fantasy at all to imagine a bunch of the boys, drunk at the local bar, getting bored and deciding to go "mess up the two 'queers' who lived down the road." In the three years I was there, I heard "fag" jokes almost daily as well as many a relished tale about how so-and-so and so-and-so had beat the shit out of the fairy who worked at. . . ."

The homophobia that gets controlled into benevolent discomfort for bleeding-heart liberal heterosexuals in cities and suburbs is raw and unmitigated in rural areas. As with blacks not so long ago, gays aren't seen quite as people. Killing a "queer" is about equivalent to shooting a rabbit. But there's more to it than that; there's more hate in it.

At any rate, being dumb but not stupid, I decided early on that my survival in rural Maryland depended on my closet. But at what price?

It would be comforting to think that the rural mindset about gays is changing. But fundamentalist preachers in rural towns still call for homosexuals—abominations of God—to be locked up, burned at the stake, or mutilated. Their congregations take them seriously.

Another whole class of people not yet mentioned who have grieving to do are emerging gay teenagers. I have told several stories so far about gay men who were tormented through their school years for being "sissies." There are similar stories for girls who get labeled "dykes." Almost without exception, patients that I see recount such tales. It would be nice to think things are changing, but in fact, the torment continues.

About two years ago, I facilitated a workshop for teachers in the District of Columbia public school system to help them better understand and deal with gay students and their homophobic classmates. The horror stories they told were incredible.

Like the sixteen-year-old boy (slightly on the "effeminate" side) who was being chased around the locker room by a group of his peers who were trying to pin him face down and shove an umbrella into his rectum. They had just about succeeded when a coach just happened to walk through and intervened.

What made such stories worse was how matter-of-factly the teachers told them; they appeared to be common occurrences.

When you put all of the particulars together, the gestalt is oppression. The experience is not of moving from one particular to another; it is a constant, chronic feeling of not belonging, of being threatened and rejected.

The point is that we are not looking at some negative philosophical hypothesis on society's part that a gay person may simply disagree with and choose to ignore. We are looking at a monolithic system bent on making life for gay people as miserable as possible. It confronts the gay person at every turn. In the words of a close friend, "You live with it every minute of your life."

The whole structure of means for achieving comfort and security that is taken for granted by straight people is denied gay people. Most things that *everybody* wants in order to feel "safe and sound" are simply not attainable by homosexuals. Living without them causes tremendous anxiety. Giving that security up is exceedingly difficult. And yet this is precisely what most gay people are forced to do.

Helping gay people grieve at this level is very difficult. Giving up parental support—perhaps never being able to see parents or siblings again—is an excruciating letting go. It's like having your whole family die at once. Knowing that, almost overnight, you might lose your job if your supervisors changed or "found out" makes dreaming or planning for the future very precarious. Realizing that you could walk down a street in most cities, be identified as gay, and be beaten up or worse can make death a not-too-subliminal, ever-present companion. Hearing people hurl insults at you from passing cars, or preachers denouncing homosexuals from pulpits, the radio, or TV, or reading about the latest anathema from Rome and not being immobilized by rage or self-hate is no easy maneuver. Reading in *Newsweek* about the latest poll confirming that most of the people in the country consider you sick or immoral or despicable is not an easy burden to lift off your shoulders.

What may be hardest about helping gay people give up all of this stuff is their lack of choice about their plight. The giving-up gay people have to do doesn't begin voluntarily; most would just as soon buy into the myth and live as happily ever after as they *think* their straight counterparts are living.

In contrast, some people *choose* to buy out of the myth. People who join ashrams, for instance, know life will be hell sometimes. They know what gurus are like. They know they will have to give up most of what gave them comfort and security. But the point is nobody forced them to do it. They chose their lot.

The bottom line, of course, is that gay people just don't have a choice. Oppression is simply what gay people face when they are authentic.

Well, what do gay people do when faced with oppression? There are three common strategies: avoid it, fight it, or suffer through it. Let's look at those three options.

Avoiding the oppression usually means pretending you're not oppressed. It amounts to being stuck at the denial or bargaining stage of grieving. For gay people, it often takes the form of a closet. Unlike the two other predominant minorities discriminated against in our society—blacks and women—being gay doesn't necessarily *show*. Under a cloak of secrecy, many gay people hide and manage to build very tall houses of cards; they move into very well-appointed closets. They often come into therapy troubled by very severe neurotic behavior (e.g., depression, paranoia, phobias, alcoholism) but are indignantly affronted if you suggest that there is a link between such behavior and being in a closet. We'll see some of this in Joe's story, later on.

Another type of avoidance usually happens in the course of therapy. In the process of grieving old chains that bound, gay patients sometimes go through a period of feeling their negative self-image turn positive. It feels like the whole world is opening up. This has some dangers, as a patient named Ed discovered.

Ed had been working very hard in therapy. In the course of a year, he had grieved a lot. Together we had taken the painful trip back through an appalling childhood and adolescence. He reclaimed and wept for eighteen years of mistreatment at the hands of two very sadistic parents who catapulted him into adulthood with almost no sense of worth.

Ed looked, and cried, and went through a period of murderous rage at two people who had hurt him so deeply, who tortured him so resolutely, especially around his identity as an emerging gay person. Public humiliations, constant harassment about his homosexuality, forced trips to unenlightened psychiatrists, and hospitalizations that included electroshock aversion "therapy," all were part of the horror story he unfolded.

Slowly (like Rachel) he cried himself dry and screamed himself hoarse over most of the horror and fear he had carried with him into adulthood. And bit by bit, he came to know his own goodness and worth as he liberated himself from all of the messages he had been shackled with that were intended to destroy him (and almost did). He began to like himself, to feel powerful. For a while he was intoxicated with his sense of well-being and freedom.

I recall one session in this ebullient period in particular. Ed came in more exuberant than I'd ever seen him. He told me how good he felt. How wonderful it was to no longer feel like dirt, or a freak, or a derelict, or a sinner. The hour ended with Ed on cloud nine. He had finally freed himself from the chains of his past. The world was his.

He emerged onto the street (he told me in the next hour) and was almost immediately accosted by a group of five inner-city toughs who had pegged him as homosexual. They collared him, called him a "fag," a "fairy," a "queer," a "punk," roughed him up, took his wallet, and ran off laughing.

The next hour was a heavy one. Ed had learned in a cruel way the limits of his freedom. He came to know that he had another whole level of grieving to do. The past he had pretty well dealt with. But the present had, until then, eluded him. And he hadn't even considered the future.

It is not enough, in therapy, to help gay people transform a negative self-image into a positive one because the world into which they emerge is, quite literally, "out to get them." It's no paranoid projection; it's for real. Not only must gay people give up attachment to what might have been but wasn't, they must also let go of what might be now and isn't and what the future might have held but won't.

It is important to keep this in mind when working with gay people. It is worse than useless to harbor the illusion, let alone communicate it to the patient, that having completed therapy, the gay patient will find a way to live "happily ever after." That is foolish even if you are working with straight patients. It is frankly cruel to offer that kind of hope to a gay patient. Gay patients will ask for it. They will want to believe that if they just work hard in therapy, make the right changes in their lives, that the burden of oppression meted out to them as gay people will be lifted off their shoulders. That kind of hope you cannot offer. Your silence in the face of such verbalized hopes, painful though it may be, will, however, help the patient deeper into the abyss—which is all they will be able to see at first—but also into the bosom of God.

Another ingrained way to deal with oppression is to fight

it. But railing against the oppressor doesn't work very well either. It's being stuck at the anger state of grieving.

When I make statements like that, I usually drive gay activists up a wall. "What are you advocating?" they retort. "Should we just lay down and take it?" And, of course, being something of an activist myself, I don't mean that at all.

I'm not suggesting that gay people shouldn't protest or march or write letters or circulate petitions. The oppressed have got to speak the pain of their exile if they're going to be authentic. "To be silent when they should protest makes cowards of men."[2]

But what do you do with your anger if you lose? If you're attached to winning as opposed to genuinely speaking your pain, and you're fighting a losing battle, you may spend the rest of your days enraged. Many gay militants do.

Then there's suffering through, a very common way gay people respond to their oppression. Suffering through is being stuck at the depression stage of grieving. Another word for it is despair.

My stereotype of a gay person in this situation is the fifty-year-old male government worker who puts in his eight hours a day, lives alone in an efficiency apartment, has no gay friends, is out to no one, and whose only social or sexual outlet is having clandestine, anonymous sex in public restrooms or parks or pornographic movie houses. He has given up, all right, but it is not a giving-up that frees. It's more like a caving-in. The oppression isn't just accepted; it's totally ingested.

Avoiding it, fighting it, or suffering through it don't appear to be very helpful ways to deal with oppression. There seems to be only one way out. Deeper.

I'm suggesting that since being in exile isn't negotiable, it might as well be embraced. And since it demands such drastic givings-up, it might as well be used as an opportunity for spiritual growth. Giving-up, after all, is manna for the spiritual journey.

Crazy as that may sound, it comes down to this. If you don't have any choice about being in exile, then why not *really* be in exile? Why not affirm it with your whole heart and soul? It may not make sense. ("Why me? Lord, why me?") It may not seem fair or just. ("I didn't ask for this!") But it might just be a God-given invitation to spiritual deepening. It just might be a blessing in disguise. It just might be an opportunity.

What gay people ultimately have to give up is attachment to rejection and the need for people to affirm their wholeness and loveableness. It works like this.

If you can't get confirmation of your wholeness and your rightful place in the universe from *people* and the myth, you just have to look beyond them. You have no choice but to get it from someplace else, someplace deeper, someplace more cosmic.

If you give up denying, fighting, or wallowing in the oppression, you stop being stuck in the mud. Off you go down the road.

You begin to see that freedom and a sense of belonging aren't to be found in the myth at all. They never were. You begin to understand what Jesus meant when he said, "My kingdom is not of this world."[3]

As you begin to experience your belongingness on a cosmic level, everything seems to lighten up. It doesn't all feel so heavy. It just is. Then what people think of you or try to do to you doesn't matter so much. What matters is that you love and are loved by love. And nobody can take it away from you. Nobody. That's solid. That's real.

You begin to realize that you've got ahold of something very special. It's really what you were looking for all along. Then it dawns on you that the exile was a gift.

I'd like to tell you a story of a fellow who took that journey. He made it.

"I'm *not* oppressed," shouted a patient named Joe in response to my suggesting that he just might be. "I have a responsible job; I make $25,000 a year; I own a condo in Alexandria; I drive a Pontiac Bonneville; I wear designer clothes; I go to Europe every other year; and no one has ever yelled anything derogatory at me out of a car window."

When I probed to find out how open he was about his sexuality, he became extremely defensive and summarily dismissed the whole matter with, "That's my personal life; it's nobody's business."

That would all track very well except for the fact that Joe harbored tremendous fears (uncovered much later) that he would be "found out." His parents were getting curious about his "roommate" of five years, and his employers had given up suggesting he bring "a friend" to business dinners. He suspected they "knew." Then there was the fact that Joe did all of his socializing in bars in Baltimore so that there would be no chance of his being spotted in Washington, and his equally denied worry that he might be drinking "a bit too heavily." Finally, there were the hypertension and rashes, and the upper G.I. series that had not yet detected an ulcer. But Joe was resolutely *not* oppressed.

For Joe, getting past denial took a long time. Again and again, I held a mirror up for him to see different aspects of his life. Again and again, he refused to look. Too painful. Too much to give up. His physical symptoms increased. The ulcer was finally diagnosed. The house of cards began to crumple.

Bargaining came next. Yes, he was oppressed. But if he could just come out to a few close straight friends, that would be enough. Just realizing the oppression made it, he thought, unnecessary to actually confront the situations that were hemming him in.

Ironically (the Lord provides), at about this time, a whisper campaign about him began at his office. A secretary had noticed that his "roommate" seemed to call him every day. Good material for a scandal. He was called in by his supervisor eventually, who told him about this "malicious rumor" and assured Joe that he would pay it no heed.

Joe began frantically looking for another job—another closet to crawl into. Next time he would be more careful: no calls from his lover, enough fake dates with women to ensure his cover, a "fag" joke here and there to leave no doubt in anyone's mind. His ulcer worsened. He was hospitalized for two weeks. A showdown lurked on the horizon.

Joe passed through anger and depression fairly quickly. Perhaps it was because he had been in therapy for a year and knew what the process of grieving was about already. But it was probably more a function of being brought face to face with the choice of either giving up or dying. The house of cards had toppled and he knew it. At any rate, our next session after his return from the hospital was a landmark one. He cursed heaven and the injustice of the world. He swore revenge. And he cried.

Things changed a lot after that. Joe eventually came out at work. He wasn't fired, but he was given clear signals that he had seen his last promotion. Some co-workers shied away from him, but some were very supportive. Nobody treated him badly. His supervisor's communications became peremptory for a while and then softened some, but they've never really been the same. He still works at the same firm; it was the best option. It's a good job with good benefits. He likes the work. But it's a bittersweet situation. He must daily experience the subtle and not-so-subtle forms of oppression meted out to gay people. But it isn't intolerable.

Joe also came out to his parents and sister. It's been six months and his parents still won't speak to him. That hurts. But his sister "was cool," in his words, and had both him *and* his lover to her house for Christmas dinner (much to their parents' horror). Who knows where that all will go?

Joe now socializes in Washington. Why not? Everyone whom he feared would find out already knows. He has also become active in the local chapter of his religious denomination's gay caucus.

Is Joe happier? Hard to say. He experiences on a daily basis more of the pain of his oppression than he did before. But he also experiences more joy. Perhaps the point is that he simply experiences *more*. Now. In the present. In the world *as it is*. Many fewer games. Much less effort. Much more reality. Does that make him happier? Maybe it would be better just to say that he's glad he did it.

Joe's life as a homosexual will contain more pain than most. He will be subject to the entire spectrum of oppression sketched out in the sampler presented above. He will be "kept down" on the corporate ladder, probably tolerated at best by his parents, forced at least partially into a gay ghetto, denied legal protections, and consigned to lower salaries than his ample talents and efforts would normally command. In short, he will be forced to dwell on the outskirts of society, in that no man's land between the fertile land and the desert. Joe's therapy, then, was a journey into exile—an exile he came to embrace.

In the past month, Joe has talked a lot about not needing society's approval any more to know that God loves him as a gay person. He talks about how church and society are wrong and that, if they only stepped back and looked at what they were doing, they would see how myopic they are being. He acknowledges with a bit of sadness that he will probably never know "total freedom" as a gay person, but that living "out" and trying to help educate the church "feels good because every little bit helps."

Joe, in my estimation, has broken through to a new level of awareness. He speaks now from a spiritual plane distinctly different from his previous one. The context in which he sees his life is inestimably broader. He had acquired some measure of cosmic perspective. He has given up to life in exile, not passively, but in a way that allows him to participate much more fully in his life as it unfolds, joy and sorrow, the whole mixed bag.

The clearest indication to me of Joe's new spiritual depth is his new-found ability to love, his openness. He's a totally different person to be with now.

The first time I saw him he was rigid, defensive, and closed. His brow was perpetually furrowed; his mouth set. He felt miles away, courteous but icy cold. Now his posture is relaxed. His face is remarkably different: unselfconscious, yielding, and soft. Now he's with me when we're together—intimately with me. He's a joy to spend an hour with. Sadly for me, there probably won't be many more of them.

My work with Joe is similar in many respects to my work with most gay Christians. The ground rules are simple enough. Keeping them is frequently difficult.

The job of anyone who sets out to be a guide for those on the journey is to help patients grasp reality as deeply and broadly as they are ready to handle. It means, as I have said earlier, that the therapist must repeatedly hold a mirror up for patients to see who they really are. This is done in bits and pieces over a long period of time.

At first all patients can see is what they have established for themselves as a self-image. You invite them to look closer. They see more of themselves, some of which they like, some of which they despise and try to reject. You hold the mirror firmly. They look again and again and again. Perhaps they come to accept more, even the warts. For gay people, it includes their coming to accept and to be able to behold their sexuality.

You ask them to look again. Deeper. They notice an aura. This may be an aspect of themselves they hadn't noticed. They begin to grasp the holy, their spirits. You shift and begin using larger and larger mirrors. They begin to notice the context in which they live and have their being. Again, at first, all they will notice is the universe they have imagined. Then the aspects they hadn't noticed, both the beautiful and the ugly. For gay people, this will require looking squarely into a social milieu that oppresses them. The anguish of that must be drunk to the dregs.

Yet a larger mirror. And a larger. Until the context is infinity, eternity, the All, God. And then they perhaps just glimpse—for who can truly *grasp* the All—that they are there, miniscule perhaps, but integral parts of the cosmic puzzle, necessary parts for the puzzle to be whole, and that the All, in all of its contortions, is strangely beautiful.

Joe came to know his own goodness by looking beyond himself and society to the cosmic goodness of all that is. He learned to love by coming to accept God's universe in its totality—with all of its beauties, contortions, and contradictions. His new-found compassion and concern for church and society and his commitment to help them grow—in spite of how resolutely they will try to undo his efforts and oppress him—reflects his having struck a spiritual stratum far beneath many of his fellow human beings. As he sent his spiritual roots deeper, he tapped the fertile soil of unfathomable love. And now he is free, free to love . . . anyway, give . . . anyway.

:9
Exile for All: An Invitation

S o what about the rest of the world? Is Joe's journey possible only for people who are gay? Must you be forced down to your spiritual roots before you can tap them?

No. The very special opportunity for spiritual deepening presented to gay people is offered to nongay people in other ways. Those who seek spiritual guidance are on the same journey; those who follow a guru tread the same path. The road to enlightenment is very broad.

All you have to do is claim it. All it takes is seeing that the oppressors are oppressed, that the myth is a myth, and that the ego is a figment of our imaginations. All you have to admit (you can do it in the privacy of your home) is that we are *all* in exile and that it is crazy to pretend we are not.

Gerald May puts it this way:

> The quixotic cultural myth is that in self-control, self-determination, self-direction, self-identity and self-confidence lies the good life. Nearly every cultural institution reflects this belief. There's nothing special about psychotherapy or about antipsychotherapy, or about politics or education. All are children of the same craziness, the insanity which says self-determination is utopia.[1]

The myth is crazy-making. It might be all right to have it; the problem is that we actually believe it. It wouldn't be so bad just to build houses of cards; the trouble is that we actually try to live in them. It's crazy.

Of course, May isn't the only person who has tried to tell us about our insanity. What he and Alan Watts[2] and Ram Dass and a few others describe in a spiritual and psychological way, many other writers have been raising red flags about for a generation or two: Orwell in *1984*,[3] Toffler in *Future Shock*,[4] Huxley in *Brave New World*,[5] and Robert Heinlein in *Stranger in a Strange Land*,[6] not to mention the procession of hair-raising treatises by enlightened economists, ecologists, and social scientists. They've all tried to tell us that our insanity *is* insanity. And they have all prophesied about where our insanity leads.

The ego gone wild. Individually, we have deified our *selves;* collectively, we have created a societal *self* with whose power we've become intoxicated. And in order to feed ego's voracious appetite, we have pushed our *selves* to the brink of every possible disaster.

We harnessed the atom, and built a bomb. Now nuclear war is an ever-present specter on the horizon. But we keep building "better" bombs. Nuclear reactors include in their power packs risks of enormous consequence. But we keep feeding them uranium.

Vital natural resources like fossil fuels, metals, and petroleum will be exhausted before too long. We know it. We've even seen the start of it. Yet we continue using them as though they were limitless.

Cities reach higher and higher toward heaven. (We've gotten proficient at erecting towers of Babel.) Urban populations continue to increase. The pressures of growth have brought most major cities to the verge of bankruptcy. But it doesn't phase us. At least thirty office buildings are rising on the skyline in Washington alone.

I remember my grandmother insisting on walking because she felt cars were too dangerous. Now we are willing to pack 200–300 people in a single jetliner and catapult it through the air at 650 miles per hour.

People used to be afraid of monopolies. Now we have multinational corporations and conglomerates large enough and monolithic enough to allow those with sufficiently large egos to wield almost inconceivable amounts of power.

More protection (bombs), more power (nukes), and more money (cities), more speed (jetliners), and more control (multinationals). And why? Because we need them? Or is it just because we could?

There is a funny and crazy movie called *The Little Plant Shop*. It's about a boy who worked in the shop who tried an experiment. He crossed a Venus's flytrap with a philodendron. Well, it grew by leaps and bounds. It also had the curious ability to speak.

At first, it was content with flies. But as it got bigger and bigger, finally reaching tree proportions, its appetite increased. About all it knew how to say, in a very rasping, loud, and demanding voice, was "Feed me!"

The boy was terrified of the thing and consented to its demands for more food. (It was carnivorous, by the way.) At first it was mice, then cats, then dogs, but ultimately it wanted people. (It had a curious predilection for mailmen and prostitutes.) Down the hatch they all went, and, although it sounds gruesome, there was something absurdly funny about seeing this plant open its trap, gobble up its latest victim, and then belch.

I don't remember how it ended, but my sense of justice makes me want to believe that the plant met its demise.

We have fed our egos exceedingly well. They have developed insatiable, ever-growing appetites. We have reached the point now that whenever something is grasped as possible—height, power, protection, profit, distance, speed, or concentration—it is automatically interpreted by our egos as necessary. It's insane.

We have built our houses of cards to enormous heights. We have learned clever ways to brace and arrange them so that (under most circumstances) they don't fall. A little super glue here. A paper clip there. And the things stand. But, my God, so precariously.

We try to convince ourselves that our constructs are indestructible. Rhetoric, treaties, insurance—even God—are invoked to try to allay our anxieties. Of course, our sanity nags us at some subliminal level, telling us that we are acting crazy. But we've become proficient at blocking those messages out; ego doesn't want to hear them.

Occasionally, God sends us poignant little reminders of our craziness, like the Soviet Union invading Afghanistan. All of a sudden, we see before us the possibility of Russia seizing all the oil fields in the Middle East. We imagine life without oil. Our defenses weaken for a moment and we glimpse our playing-card skyscrapers crashing down around our ears. The prospect is terrifying.

We experience the terror, all right. But what we usually cannot see is that we set it up. The dimensions of the potential disaster are precisely proportionate to our insatiable desire to grab more, have more, make more, and control more.

What we ultimately do with one of God's little reminders is defend ourselves. Protect more. Insure more. Insulate more. Sign more treaties. Become more self-sufficient. Never, never do we hear the voice of sanity saying, "Why not take a few floors off the top, guys?"

A few of us loons sit on the sidelines, watching the latest skyscraper go up, more or less quietly muttering, "But, you know, we basically control nothing." Old sayings like, "The bigger they are, the harder they fall," run through our heads. But nobody listens to fools.

And for those of us loony enough, psychotherapy becomes a chosen profession. The choice is loony because, unlike the days of yore, it is almost impossible to know what the work of psychotherapy *is* nowadays.

Once it was easy. In the days when the social order was clear and dominant, the therapist's job was clear, too: reintegrate patients back into the order.

As the order has turned into chaos, however, therapists have been yanked in every possible direction as they attempt to figure out which flag to follow in which parade. A once unified profession has turned into a mass jumble of anything-but-unified schools and techniques and methods all trying to grab onto something concrete to use as a basis for doing the work. I don't claim to be an exception.

But one thing hasn't changed. People still come through the door saying, "I'm broken. Fix me. Get me back in the game, coach." Then you have a choice. You either sigh, say, "Sure, kid!" do your razzle-dazzle, and get them back out there on the field so that they can dog-eat-dog themselves to death. Or, you can introduce them to themselves as they really are: infinitesimal and ultimately powerless expressions of almighty God, or Cosmic Being, or the Force.

If psychotherapy is seen as a process of helping patients examine and correct their distorted or inadequate maps of the cosmos, if psychotherapy is committed to helping patients increase their perception of reality—of the world as it really is—and begin living in that world, then those of us whose world view embraces the concepts and experience of life presented here cannot help but approach *all* patients the same way.

Many of them will leave. "This way is too hard," they will say. "He was nice but crazy." Or maybe, "I swear he comes from another planet. I decided to try someone more 'traditional.'"

More likely, patients will stay long enough to get what they came for and *then* leave. They will stay until the crisis has passed, or until, in the process of affirming some piece of their ego (what happens before they get to give it up), they get to feeling their oats. They will decide they are fixed then and leave. There is nothing to do about it. It is as far as they can go. They will return to the field invigorated, convinced that they are all better, and get back into the skyscraper business.

But it is always possible for everyone to go further—deeper. And to go deeper into the reality of what is inevitably leads away from the self, away from the power-hungry ego, toward a more comprehensive map of the cosmos, one that ultimately makes an anthropocentric world view impossible.

As we look more and more closely at the unfathomable complexity of the universe and begin to comprehend its e-normity, we cannot but begin to feel inconsequential and pow-erless. We begin to notice that the *dis-coveries* of science, for instance, are nothing more than the word literally means: "the uncovering of truths or wonders *that were there all along*." Discovery does not mean creation.

If we could get loose of the egocentric need to praise our-selves for making the find (with Nobel prizes and the like), we might open ourselves to the wonder of the universe, whose creation and ordering were and are totally beyond us.

A popular song sung by Barbra Streisand mourns the loss of that kind of wonder.

> Where is the wonder that I once felt
>   watching snowflakes melt as a child?
> Where is the wonder that I once knew
>   when a sky of blue turned wild?
> Where is the magic that thrilled me so
>   watching flowers grow in the spring?
> Where are the marvels that I marvelled at?
>   What changed a kitten to a cat?
> Where are the mysteries that I couldn't solve?
>   What made the world revolve?
> Where is the wonder that years conceal,
>   that a child can feel now and then?
> O, where is the wonder of long ago,
>   that I'll never know again.[7]

A child has not learned so much to try to control the universe. A child's smallness and lack of information allows more for wonder, for a sense of infinitesimalness and powerlessness. A child's ego hasn't taken over yet. It will soon enough.

It is not impossible for adults to reclaim such wonder, but it is a hard journey. As the last line of the song would suggest, many have given up trying forever. The ego is so damned tenacious.

Even if we do resolve to let go of control, we are likely to want to give up only some of it. Perhaps we'll be willing to look at the universe *out there* and acknowledge, if reluctantly, that we are only a few sentient beings among several billion sentient beings on one planet of nine in one solar system among trillions of solar systems in *what we know* of the universe. Perhaps we will embrace our macrocosmic powerlessness. But then there is the cosmos inside.

"Well, at least I can control *my* life and *my* self," we say. And we try. Chapter 2 looked at how resolutely we try to control our destinies. We don't want to look at how much of our lives is shaped by forces outside of our control: death, departure, illness, injury, the change of a boss, the bankruptcy of a firm, cutbacks, layoffs, changes in "the market," or a child who becomes quite other than expected. And how about intrapsychically? The analysts contend that ninety-five percent of what we do arises out of the unconscious. They're probably right. How much of what we choose is truly choosing?

It seems as though we're all pretty powerless right across the board. When we take a tour through all the nooks and crannies of the cosmic map—if we dare to look and experience—we can't help but be overwhelmed. The tension that this sense of "not being in control"—*angst*—creates in us is the common denominator of all our exiles: gay or straight, male or female, black or white.

So far, you've seen some evidence for believing that the exile is accessible to all of us. I've also painted a rather bleak picture suggesting that if we don't all start embracing the exile, our power-hungry, reality-denying egos may do us in. You might call that a scare tactic.

The problem with scare tactics is that, by themselves, they don't work. (Look at presidential attempts at voluntary wage and price controls.) The reason they don't work is that it's hard to convince anyone to give something up unless there's a payoff. Unless people can perceive that there is something positive to be gained by giving up the myth, they won't. I have no doubt that we are capable of blowing ourselves into oblivion. After all, who would believe how far we've let our insanity progress already?

This chapter is subtitled "An Invitation." Not much has been said so far about why anyone would find embracing this fundamental anxiety of human existence inviting at all. It's time to say something on the positive side. Let's begin with a story.

I'd like to introduce you to a patient named Jane. Jane was in her late forties, married, and the mother of four children. She came to therapy because everything was wrong. Her kids weren't turning out right. Her husband was growing distant. She was a bored housewife. And so on. As a result of it all, she was feeling very anxious and expressed it either by withdrawing and sulking or by having violent outbursts of anger, the origin of which we couldn't trace.

Jane and I began exploring the cosmos together, comparing what we saw with what her distorted, impoverished map of the cosmos indicated. We had been at it for months. My task during this phase was fairly clear and repetitive. Jane would take some aspect of her life and proceed to package it nicely in her mind and stuff it in a cubbyhole. My role for a while was always to notice a little piece that was still sticking out. In the process of fixing that, more pieces of her life would come tumbling out. Then she would frantically set about packaging those up and stuffing them in cubbyholes. Ironically, I always managed to find some piece of each of them that just didn't quite fit. As you can guess, it was a geometric progression. In a sense, I had designed the game that way. Jane's game was compulsive control. Unless she gave it up, she would continue her descent into misery. My tactic was to encourage her compulsion, but to entice her into a game that she ultimately had to lose. But in losing, she would win.

At every turn, things seemed to get more convoluted. At one point, she dishearteningly commented, "Every time I go to get a handle on something in here, it either vanishes or ends up opening another can of worms." But we continued exploring.

She got more and more frustrated in her desperate search to find something—anything—that she could set in concrete.

Finally, during one session marked by her utter despair, she threw up her hands and exclaimed, "The hell with it! It's too much! I give up!" And she slumped back in her chair.

It wasn't true, of course. Jane wasn't really ready to give up yet. She regained her resolve and went on exploring for handles for a good long time to come. It took many turns of the merry-go-round before she began *really* giving up.

But beginning with this session, she began little by little to relax her grip on things. At first it was, "Damn kids, they'll do what they want no matter what you say. You'd think I wanted her (a daughter) to go to college for *me*. (In fact, that's exactly what I thought.) This would soften later to "Lord, I guess she'll have to learn the *hard* way," with still a healthy dose of resentment in her voice. Finally, I was told, "You know, it's *her* life. She's got to live it as she sees it. It's all I can do to keep up with my own." "You've figured out that you can't control her?" I asked. "Control *her*?" Jane retorted with a smile. "Hell, I can't control *anything*!" "You seemed to enjoy saying that," I responded, smiling too. "I don't know about enjoying it," Jane replied, scrunching up her face into a quizzical grimace, "but it sure is a relief."

Working through the relationship with her daughter became a paradigm for Jane as she worked through her relationships with many of the other people and components of her life. Ultimately came her relationship with her self. "If I can't control anybody or anything else, I guess I'll just have to be responsible for *me*," she exclaimed definitively one day. "How do you mean *responsible*?" I asked. "Self-control," she responded proudly. "I can control *me*."

As you can guess, a lot more exploring followed. And a once obsessively compulsive housekeeper became—for a while—a slob (much to the children's delight and her spouse's bafflement). A once tied-to-the-stove housewife decided to try a part-time job, which became a career, and now the cleaning woman comes once a week. A woman who was once programmed to the hilt, from dawn to dusk, now enjoys just walking in the woods behind her home "when the Spirit moves me," as she says.

There is still a lot of pain in Jane's life. Life itself got no easier as she changed her attitude toward it. Her husband isn't at all pleased with her career. He wants her back in the kitchen where she belongs. Her daughter did not, in fact, go to college. She became an unwed mother on welfare instead, and is having a hell of a time. Jane's boredom with being a housewife has now been replaced by the frustration of being a woman with fine skills in a male-dominated misogynist profession.

At one point, I asked her how she would compare her life now with how it used to be. She responded, "Well, it isn't any easier, if that's what you mean. No fewer problems. No smoother sailing. But I don't let it get to me as much. I don't fight it so much. If I'm feeling overwhelmed, hell, I just let myself *be* overwhelmed. I don't feel as though I'm spending so much energy worrying. Which is nice, because when good things happen—and don't misunderstand me, they do—I'm not so preoccupied with worrying that I can't enjoy them."

Changing the externals of her life didn't bring Jane to nirvana. But giving up trying to acquire nirvana has gotten her a lot closer. She has learned something about living in the present, not grasping for "handles," but gently taking whatever comes to hand. She has gone a long way toward giving up her cherished wish that life be eternally blissful, peaceful, and orderly, and has decided to take life as it comes—all of it.

The only sensible reason why anyone would choose to embrace rather than run from anxiety so profound and so pervasive is that, ultimately, it is easier.

There are two steps in coming to believe this. The first one involves getting comfortable with anxiety.

Anxiety is viewed as a bad thing by most people. It is, after all, one of those feelings of weakness that does not compute in the mythic program. Ironically, many patients come to therapy precisely to be "cured" of their anxiety. Even more ironic is that, if the therapy is successful, what they truly end up doing is learning how to *tolerate* it.

People anticipate therapy with all of the dread of a person

going to a dentist to have root canal work done. They are braced against all of their worst fears, heightened by the experiences other people have shared with them about how awful it is. They frequently find out that the process is just as awful as they expected.

At the same time, they learn that pain is not the end of the world, that they don't die of it, and that it is unavoidable. They come to know that the experience of pain isn't half as bad as the dread of it. In other words, the *idea* of pain gets cut down to size.

This is communicated to patients in a variety of ways, some subtle and some not so subtle. By truly empathizing with a patient's pain *without making any gestures to save them from it*, the therapist lets the patient know that the patient's pain is his or her own. It communicates an inevitability about pain. Sometimes, in response to a patient's recounting of pain it is helpful to share a similar piece of your own, not with this underlying message, "You think *you* have it tough! Well I . . . ," but with the message, "I hear your pain. I know it hurts. I've had pain like that, too. We each have our pain. There's no way to avoid it."

There are times when I am more direct. "I can't stand the pain," said a patient. "Yes you can," I replied. "I think it's going to kill me," she went on, desperately trying to manipulate me into saving her. "The hell of it is that it probably won't," I replied. "You're a heartless son-of-a-bitch!" she screamed. "We established that months ago," I replied, smiling wryly. We exchanged glances. The patient smirked. "You know, for a shrink, you are really a horse's ass."

The clincher is that patients end up walking out the door carying the same life burden they walked in with and wanted to unload. But there's a difference now. They've given up fighting it, or trying to dump it on someone, or run from it. There it sits squarely on their own shoulders and—guess what?—they don't crumple under like they thought they would.

The immediate experience of letting go into the angst of the human condition is relief. However grudging the letting go has been, it's followed by a feeling of "God, I'm glad that's over." What is *over*, of course, is not the anxiety, but all of the frenetic, futile, and energy-draining activity formerly engaged in to try to avoid the anxiety. As you give up trying to control this or insure that or develop a surefire plan for thus and so, life gets immeasurably easier. You find that there is energy to spare.

It is this spare energy that becomes the springboard for actually embracing the exile. Energy that isn't consumed in death dealing, controlling, and manipulative activity is free to be used creatively, here and now, in the present. Life gets airy and colorful. Sometimes the colors are painful to look at; sometimes ecstatically joyous. But either way, they are vibrant.

To the extent that we aren't trying to control or manipulate or exploit people, we're free to behold them, be fascinated by them, love them—in all of their wickedness and virtue. To the extent that we aren't bent on raping the environment, we can *be* with it, revel in it, glory in it, and fear it. Insofar as we give up needing to be the center of the universe, we're free to stand in awe of it and be entranced by it, both its destructive aspect and its generative one. If we can just give up to the surging power of life, we can be empowered by it.

What you're being invited to consider is that the spiritual depths down to which gay people are often thrust isn't such a bad place to be. In fact, it may be the only sane place *to* be. A blessing. A blessing I'm sure gay people would be willing to share with any sanity-seeking heterosexuals.

I noticed a curious thing about a year ago: straight people who have traveled a while on the spiritual path are remarkably untroubled by a gay person's sexuality. It is simply a nonissue for them. I liked that, of course, when it occurred to me, but I didn't understand it. I needed to travel a while on the path myself first.

The understanding came during a group meditation. There were eight of us. We were in someone's living room. It was dusk. We were just sitting there in silence, a candle burning at the hub of our circle.

For a moment I slipped out of the deep stillness I had been in. It surprised me a little, but there was a freshness about it, rather like just waking up from a restful sleep. So I just sat there, expecting nothing, quietly enjoying the vibrancy of the moment, open to whatever came next.

Gently, I let my mind take in the experience of us all sitting there. And quite unselfconsciously, I happened to notice that some of us were men, and some women; some straight, and some gay. I noticed, too, that I rather liked us all being there, sitting together, quietly, in a circle.

Just as I began to slip back into the peaceful stillness of my meditation, it all made sense.

When you are sitting and looking into the face of the Mystery, when you are overcome with awe and gratitude and joy for the overwhelming everythingness of God, and you feel like an empty vessel being filled to overflowing with love, the sexual preference of the person next to you is just nothing. It doesn't matter at all. What matters is that you are both there, looking, worshiping, and being loved by love. Anything else is a distraction.

:10
Witches and Wizards

lmost all of what's been said so far has focused either on the patient, the journey, or the world. Not much has been said about the therapist. This chapter will take a closer look at those who choose to accompany patients on their journeys.

How do you do the kind of work described in this book? How must the therapist be? *Who* must the therapist be? And, in particular, what does it take for therapists to be helpful to gay patients?

In his book, *The Only Dance There Is*, Ram Dass contends that "Psychotherapy is just as high [enlightened] as the psychotherapist."[1] That's always bothered me.

I don't think Ram Dass is saying that patients can't become more enlightened than their therapists. I know that isn't true. But he does seem to be claiming that the therapist can only be helpful until patients reach the therapist's level of enlightenment. So if patients want to get more enlightened than their therapists, they either have to find a more enlightened therapist or go it alone. That one has troubled me.

On the one hand, I've wanted to disagree. If therapists stuck to doing the work well, I thought, couldn't they help patients explore *anything*, no matter how deep or different from their own experience? Sort of like blue-collar parents who send their kids off to college and support them as they develop sophistication and a breadth of experience that the parents themselves will never approach. It's a little sad getting left behind, but they love their kids enough to want the best for them.

On the other hand, that seemed simplistic. Although blue-collar parents may be willing to support and bless the kids on their journey, they really can't be very helpful in guiding them once they set out. "Hey, dad," says a son to his machine shop foreman father, "do you think I should take macroeconomics or third world political systems this semester?" What's the man to say? Is there some way in which therapists have to tread the path their patients are embarked on in order to be useful guides?

I eventually realized that this was just another instance of wrestling with the psychological-spiritual split. Perhaps therapists who confine their work to developing egos *can* help patients develop ego strength even greater than their own. I don't know. But what traditional therapists absolutely *can't* do is help patients explore the spiritual strand of the double helix; they can't help them give up any part of their egos. To the extent that therapists have bought into the myth, they can't help patients buy out of it.

Of course, it's not an all or nothing proposition; it's a continuum. Another look at the double helix will make that clear.

If you'll recall, the psychospiritual journey seems to involve a back and forth rhythm upward between the strands of the double helix. It always arises with something ego-affirming on the psychological strand and then reaches fruition through giving it up (transcending it) on the spiritual strand. There's a jump involved, a leap (of faith?) from the psychic strand to the spiritual one.

What follows, then, is that therapists can't help patients take the leap on any level of the helix beyond where they have lept themselves. That doesn't mean patients can't surpass their therapists in spiritual growth. It only means the therapists can't help them do it.

An example. Let's invent a therapist named John. John has progressed to the point of giving up his need for power. He used to be manipulative, controlling, and compulsive; now he takes life more as it comes. But he still needs a lot of self-affirmation. (His ego still needs to be assured of its identity.) He meets this need in several ways. He seeks out praise from his colleagues. He prides himself on having a good reputation in the community. And he works hard at "getting published."

One of John's patients begins saying things like, "You know, I'm really not so concerned any more about what people think of me. I know who I am and that's enough."

That kind of statement tells *me* that the patient might be on the verge of a real spiritual breakthrough. But John can't hear it that way; it's too threatening to his ego. So he falls into countertransference and says, "You're really frustrated with people putting you down. You'd just as soon block out hearing them reject you. But deep down, you know you need their affirmation." The patient scratches his head and says, "Yeah, I guess you're right," and a possibility of a jump to the spiritual strand is nipped in the bud.

To that extent, I agree with Ram Dass. Therapists can't help patients get any more *spiritually* enlightened than they are themselves.

This has a lot of implications for both how therapists need to be and what training they need in order to do good work. Let's look at some specific attributes therapists are commonly assumed to need. Take, for example, empathy.

Empathy is defined as "mental entering into the feeling or spirit of a person . . . ; appreciative perception or understanding. . . ."[2] Empathy, then, isn't defined as a skill, but as a way of being; the word describes a state of consciousness.

Empathy has been warped to mean many things in therapeutic circles. Most of the time, it's been watered down or trivialized to mean only a kind of behavior. But Carl Rogers, who coined the term in its therapeutic sense, is very clear about what he does and doesn't mean by empathy.

> I hope the above account of an empathic attitude will make it abundantly clear that I am not advocating a wooden technique of pseudo-understanding in which the counselor "reflects back what the client has just said." I have been more than a little horrified at the interpretation of my approach

which has sometimes crept into the teaching and training
of counselors.[3]

Rogers, then, draws a clear distinction between a feigned attitude and an actual level of consciousness. When he uses the
word *empathy*, he doesn't mean a professional facade erected
for the duration of the therapeutic hour. Therapists aren't
supposed to *pretend* to be empathic as if it were a technique;
they have to *be* empathic.

In light of this, Carkhuff's[4] training program, which has
counselors practice "empathic responses," misses the mark.
If counselors *are* empathic, they will naturally respond to
patients empathically. If counselors *aren't* empathic, their responses will be phony, and patients can always see through
phoniness.[5] They may never be able to verbalize it, but they'll
know.

I remember a talk I had with my organ professor at Oberlin
about how people with no musical training can tell the difference between good and bad performances. He put it this
way: "They may never be able to say what they disliked about
a bad performance. They may not even be able to say that it
was bad. But they'll respond appropriately. They just won't
come back."

The same is true for therapy. Patients may never be able
to say, "The therapist was a phony." They'll just leave.

Another common (and Rogerian) attitude considered essential for doing good therapy is "unconditional positive regard."[6] It's the same story here. Rogers again means that
therapists must really, under any circumstance, *feel* positively
toward patients. Not pretend to be nonjudgmental, even
though you think they're obnoxious. Not liking who they are
deep down but hating all the rest. *Unconditional positive regard* means "it's totally all right with me that you are·just the
way you are right now." How can you fake it? The therapist
either feels that way toward a patient or doesn't.

What does it take to *be* empathic and feel unconditional
positive regard? Simple: It takes a very profound spirituality.
To actually enter into the spirit of another person, to be totally
with him, to honest-to-God experience what it's like to *be* him

from inside, you have to get out of your *self*. You have to transcend your *self*.

To unconditionally let a person be, no holds barred—*all* of him—requires a consciousness that takes *everything* as it is. If you need to define patients' behaviors, feelings, and thoughts as either right or wrong, sick or healthy, productive or unproductive, constructive or destructive, you aren't there. You've got to take it all just as it is and be able to say with all your heart, "Yes." No shoulds. No musts. No betters. No worses. "It all, just simply, is."[7] *That's* unconditional positive regard.[8]

Empathy and unconditional positive regard are held up as the cornerstones of most humanistic therapies. They are attitudes considered essential for therapists to do good work. So you would expect that spiritual formation would be a staple in clinical training programs. But it isn't.

Therapists-in-training often come at the whole pursuit convinced that they have empathy and unconditional positive regard as natural gifts. "Of course I can be empathic! Of course I can accept anything a patient says!" These attitudes are simplistically assumed to be the "raw material" from which therapists are made. What aspiring therapists really need is *technique*. At least, that's the common assumption.

Of course, what aspiring young helpers usually come bearing to their training is sympathy ("I can enter into your spirit as long as it's just like mine.") and pietistic goodwill (do-gooder-ism). The delusion usually persists until therapists see their first character disorder. They pick a little at the patient's defenses and the patient begins to attack: "You think you're so bloody smart because you're a professional, don't you?" 'What makes you think you're worth $40 an hour?" "You dress like a slob." "I feel like the whole year we've been together was a waste." "You're as haughty and cold as my father." Then it's not so easy to be empathic and feel unconditional positive regard. Sympathy and pietism turn easily into icy self-righteousness when not accepted with adulation.

When the journey gets tough, patients will ferret our therapists' weak points, the places where their egos are still attached. Patients will go after those places with a pickax. The

more attached therapists are to their own stuff, the less able
they will be either to enter into patients' spirits or accept
them as they are. Ego-bound therapists will either act out
themselves in the therapy or withdraw into a detached, chilly
therapeutic posture. Either way it's countertransference.
Either way, the work doesn't get done.

To the extent that therapists have gotten free of their egos,
they can be empathic and positively regarding. If there isn't
any self, then there's nothing to lose. Patients can attack all
they like, but because there is really no self to attack,[9] there
is nothing to defend.

Therapists can then concentrate on being in their patients'
heads, trying to get in tune with what it is like for them to
be acting the way they are, how it must feel, and what it
means for them. It is also possible, then, to totally accept the
way they are being. Why not? The therapist has nothing at
stake.

I would define this way of being with patients as "loving."
This raises a lot of hackles among therapists. Many can't
fathom the idea of love in a "professional" relationship. I'm
proposing the exact opposite: therapists have to be "professional lovers."

In his book, *The Road Less Travelled*, M. Scott Peck defines
love as: "The will to extend one's self for the purpose of nurturing . . . another's spiritual growth."[10] I agree with him as
far as the purpose is concerned. I think he misses something
important by using the word *extend*. Peck is still tied to ego
concepts like *cathecting* or reaching out with one's self to *take
in* someone else. I would use the word *transcend*. Love means
"transcending one's self for the purpose of nurturing . . . another's spiritual growth." Therapists are professionals committed to transcending their *selves* (giving up their ego
attachments) for the purpose of nurturing another's spiritual
growth. Therapists are professional lovers.

Sheldon Kopp has this to say about love in the therapeutic
relationship: "Unless the therapist comes to love his patients,
all he will do is teach them new tricks."[11] I would interpret
Kopp's words this way: "Unless the therapist gets free of his

own ego attachments and selflessly nurtures his patients, all he will do is train patients to have the same ego attachments as his own." Which sounds very much like, "Therapists can't help patients get any more spiritually enlightened than they are themselves."

It's true that therapists' own spiritual deepening frees them to love their patients and do the work. But there's another reason for therapists to work on their own enlightenment: the corrective nature of the therapeutic relationship. Patients come to accept all of who they are and to claim their rightful place in the cosmos because they come to believe, often slowly and painfully, that the *therapist* sees them that way. Thomas Hora put it this way:

> Our therapeutic task is to lift [a patient] out of [his] habitual ways of perceiving [himself] to realize that [he] is fully entitled to be a wholesome, free individual who is a beneficial presence in the world. . . .[12]

I remember in my own therapy that my most important breakthroughs came when I could know and accept my therapist's love for me.

I remember in particular the session when I decided (finally) to face into some very painful old material about my parents. I had avoided it for more than a year. My therapist had given me opportunities to explore the material on many occasions—always gently, never forcefully. She would point to it when it came up and then let me decide to look or not look. For a year, I refused. Not directly. I never said, "I don't want to look at that." But I did manage to skirt a large chunk of the pain surrounding my relationship with my parents through evasion, by dismissing it as unimportant, or by choosing some piece of it that was less threatening.

During this one session, though, I moved past that barrier and began dealing head-on with some of the most painful stuff I had explored so far. That in itself, despite the agony, was rewarding.

But what I was struck by much more was her loving patience. As I sat there, the entire year's worth of her gentle encouragements—encouragements without coercion—passed through my mind. I recalled how acceptingly she had let me skirt what I wasn't willing to look at. And I was overwhelmed by how much she loved me to have waited so long for me to do what I needed to do.

Her willingness to let me be was unconditional; she was willing to walk beside me on my journey, gently suggesting ways to turn, but was perfectly content to let me take detours, walking beside me still, without resentment.

When I perceived the enormity of her love for me, I wept uncontrollably. When I could pull myself together enough to say how loved I felt by her patience, she simply said, "You weren't ready." More acceptance. And I wept all the more.

But there was another corrective aspect to this event. My coming to know how much I was loved by *her* served as a foil for claiming how much I felt *unloved* by my parents. I had already decided to face into that pain. But this overwhelming presence of love dredged up all the years absent of love. I could then let myself be overwhelmed with my grief. It was safe. I knew she would be there. After all, she loved me.

Love, of course, doesn't always get delivered in such pretty packages. Sometimes it's like being put on the rack. Here is an example.

At one point in my marriage, my spouse and I were going through some stormy times. We decided to do some work together, with both of our therapists.

During one session, I was really rattling on about how badly he had treated me in some instance. On and on I went, spouting off about how rotten he'd been, how badly I'd been hurt, and how innocent I was.

Sooner or later, I took a breath. And in that little, innocuous gap, his therapist interjected, "You really relish your resentments, don't you?" There was nothing accusatory about how she said it. She just said it.

I felt as though a ton of bricks had fallen on my head. I felt like a fish that had been hooked and flipped out of the water; I was plummeting through the air. I felt like the bottom had fallen out of my world. I sat there paralyzed.

When I came to, I saw red. I hated her. I wanted to kill her. She was Katashaw from the *Mikado*. She was the Wicked Witch of the West from the *Wizard of Oz*. I had nightmares about her. I stormed for a week. I said I wouldn't go back.

Eventually, I tuckered myself out. And when I finally got off my broom, I realized that she was absolutely right. When I stopped fighting it, her comment allowed me to let go of a major piece of what was binding me. I *did* relish my resentments. I hung onto them. I hoarded them. I filed them away. I pulled them out as ammunition when I was fighting. And I truly did enjoy the whole business. I didn't much like owning it, but it was a major factor in what was causing havoc in my marriage. And, after all, that's what I went there to work on.

Her interjection was the most loving thing she could have said. She was genuinely empathic—she had entered into my spirit and succinctly understood what my behavior meant for me. And she was regarding me in a totally positive way—it was perfectly all right with her for me to harbor resentments. She was just doing her job, commenting on it.

Ultimately, this incident had a corrective effect, too. First, it helped me see that sometimes, when people say things to me I don't like, they aren't out to get me. They may in fact be loving me. That, then, put me intimately in touch with a childhood with parents who more often than not *were* out to get me and who almost did me in. Also, when I came to accept in myself what she was willing to accept, namely, my need to harbor resentments, I didn't need to do it so much any more.

What happens *between* the therapist and the patient is every bit as important as what patients eventually do with the material they uncover. The relationship is the primary vehicle through which patients come to embrace who they are and claim their rightful place in creation. If the therapist is not free enough to truly enter into the spirit of the patient and then love them unconditionally, this part of the work never gets done.

What are the implications of this whole train of thought on working with gay people?

Well, one conclusion is uncontestable. Homophobic thera-
piste can't help homosexuals. It's ridiculous to imagine entering into the spirit of a gay person and truly understanding
their experience from the inside if you are uncomfortable with
or revulsed by homosexuality. To illustrate this, take a hypothetical male therapist who is subliminally squeamish
about the idea of anal sex between men. He will never be able
to empathize with a gay man telling him how satisfying and
meaningful and important that is to him. The therapist may
hear the words, but there won't be any empathy.

The same is true of unconditional positive regard. If therapists do not, in fact, feel or think that homosexuality "just
is," that it is neither bad nor good, healthy nor sick, but is
simply a part of the cosmos, they will never be able to love
gay patients (*all* of them) and help them grow. Let me give
you a hair-raising example.

I began seeing a thirty-eight-year-old man named Brian
about a year ago who had been in analysis for eight years. He
was the most depressed patient I had ever seen. He sat list-
lessly and wrang his hands session after session. He also lifted
his arms repeatedly, and dropped them in his lap to punctuate
his utter desperation in trying to make sense of his life. He
had no social life and spent almost every evening alone at
home, wallowing in depression and self-pity.

Along with depression, his characterological defenses made
the vault at Fort Knox look like a pup tent. Disdainful and
cynical, he seemed to imply that nothing I could say was
"right." Every statement I made was met with something like
"No, that's not even close," or "Christ, man, why don't you
say something *helpful?*"

I was baffled, especially since the analyst Brian had seen
was someone quite famous. Surely, *some* work had to have
been done in their time together. But as I kept looking at this
contorted human being before me, I found myself asking,
"What the hell did they *do* for eight years?"

Brian shed some light on the situation soon enough. The
analyst was a neo-Freudian who quite explicitly refused to
accept that Brian was constitutionally homosexual. Any homosexual productions that Brian made were automatically

interpreted as evidence of intrapsychic conflict that needed to be resolved. Once resolved, the analyst assured him, Brian would be heterosexual.

Brian believed him. After all, the analyst was the expert. And what the analyst's homophobia produced was eight years of futility. By the time Brian got to me, not only did he have most of his therapeutic agenda to work through, but he also had the rage of having "wasted eight years" and "blown $50,000" to grieve about.

Brian came to see (it took a while) that the time and expense hadn't *all* been a waste. The analytic work really had been done. Brian had learned more in eight years about his infancy, childhood, and adolescence and their connection to his current attitudes and behavior than any four of us need to know in a lifetime. But, overdone as it was, that cognitive groundwork did allow the therapy to move more quickly.

Within two months, simply because I truly regarded his gayness as a rightful and authentic part of who he was, Brian changed dramatically. He got involved in the Gay Community Center, he started dating, his depression lifted, the hand-wringing stopped, and the defenses all but disappeared. Most of it was an uphill climb. It was hard for him to give up the old, familiar ways. But he did.

In another four months, Brian wanted to quit. I think he had more stuff to look at (and he may be back) but, after eight years of being stuck, he felt so much better that he was ready to try it on his own.

Therapists who want to treat gay people must have traveled a long way down the spiritual path. Since gay people, thrust down by oppression to their spiritual roots, need more spiritual nurturance than straight people, therapists who work with gay people need to have struck their own spiritual roots deep, too. If they are to help gay people transcend society's too narrow view of reality, they must have transcended that view themselves.

What does all of this say about training for therapists? Well, the writing seems to be on the wall. What therapists need more than anything else is to work on themselves. In Hora's words, "The most important aspect of training, it would seem, is the liberation of the therapist's consciousness."[13] More will be said later about technique, but the truth of the matter is that, all the technique in the world is worthless if therapists haven't taken their own painful journeys through the valley of darkness. Therapists' own spiritual maturity is the unnegotiable cornerstone of their qualifications.

How therapists take that journey is often a matter of style. Intensive psychotherapy with a spiritually enlightened therapist is one way. (As it happens, my therapist was also an Episcopal priest; the spiritual dimension of our work was often explicit.) Supervision with an enlightened practitioner is another. Seeking spiritual direction, studying Zen or Yoga (but not just *hatha*—body work—Yoga), or other types of spiritually oriented meditations are other ways. Finding a guru, joining an ashram for a while, or making regular visits to religious retreat houses are still other possibilities. And then practicing—for the rest of their lives.

Some of the above may sound esoteric (I don't imagine many therapists will run off to ashrams) but what seems more unfathomable to me is that it is possible at present, in all fifty states, for someone to be licensed as a psychiatrist, a clinical psychologist, or a psychiatric social worker without ever having had *a day* of personal therapy of *any* kind, let alone a spiritually oriented variety.

Therapists can't help patients get any more spiritually enlightened than they are themselves. And anyone on the path will confirm that enlightenment doesn't happen automatically. If, in fact, a therapist's own level of consciousness is a primary qualification for doing good work, then it is unconscionable for licensing boards to totally ignore that aspect of a prospective therapist's training.

Where does technique fit into all of this? Another incident from my Oberlin days taught me about the rightful place of technique.

I remember repeatedly getting very annoyed with my organ professor when he would stop me to correct a note error. As far as I was concerned, it was making *music* that was important. It was the *soul* of the thing that made it music—the movement, the flow, the feeling. Notes were incidental annoyances.

Now, some of my overreaction was understandable. Most organists at Oberlin were so preoccupied with technical perfection that they never made any music at all. I was often struck, after a dry, metronomic—but absolutely accurate—performance, that a computer could have done the same thing.

One day, however, having just been corrected for an "F" where an "A" should have been, I complained. "You didn't say anything about how well I phrased that passage or how free and alive it felt! All you could notice was a wrong note! It's the music that's important! The soul of it!" My professor chuckled. Then he smirked, furrowed his brow, and said, "Look, my zealous friend, you're forgetting something. The *music* you want to make—the *soul*, as you say—comes through a medium. The medium *is* the notes. If you hit a wrong one, you may be making *something*, but you're not making *music*, at least not *this* music," and he pointed to the score. "The soul must come first," he went on, "but the technique must follow, and it must be impeccable." Well, that shut me up.

It's the same for psychotherapy. The soul (the love, empathy, and unconditional positive regard) must come first (in preeminence, not necessarily in time) but the technique must follow. And it has to be impeccable. Just as technique is worthless without spiritual depth (as demonstrated by some of my peers at Oberlin who played like machines and by any number of very cold, analytic therapists) spiritual depth is worthless in therapy unless you can convey it through the medium. It is a medium made up of reflections of feelings, confrontations, structural questioning, interpretations, and silence. Knowing *how* to use each of these skills and knowing *when* to use them *is* the work. It's got to be done impeccably.

I'd like to offer one last thought on technique. It has to do with transference in the therapeutic relationship.

In traditional analytic work, the transference is treated a certain way. The patient projects onto the therapist either positive or negative feelings of one sort or another. The roots

of those projections are usually found in significant relationships and events in the patient's history. The therapist's re
sponse to the transference is to redirect the feelings back to
the patient's intrapsychic stuff. "You get angry with me when
I don't answer your questions. I'll bet that's how you used to
react when your father didn't pay attention to you."

A few analytic psychotherapists (notably Robert Langs) reverse the process. The patient comes in and says, "I've had
a terrible week. My boss chewed me out for something I didn't
do. My wife complained because I had to work late. It seems
like nobody understands me." Langs responds, "I hear you
telling me that you don't feel I understand you."

What this does is to draw the patient into the transference.
It encourages the transference. If you do it consistently, it
funnels *all* the patient's stuff into the transference. The relationship then becomes *very* intense. It tries the therapist's
spiritual depths as no other approach can.

Sheldon Kopp incorporates much of Langs's technique into
his work. He also uses Yoga as a metaphor for psychotherapy.
And there is a striking similarity between how Kopp works
and how a guru operates.

Disciples run the gamut of feelings for their gurus from
adoration to detestation. There are many Eastern stories
about tumultuous relationships between gurus and chelas
(like the one about Marpa and Milarepa in Chapter 5). They
reveal at least one way that gurus help disciples toward enlightenment. In Western terms, the guru draws the chela into
a highly charged transferential relationship. For a while, the
chela's whole world becomes the guru. All of the ego attachments get worked out in terms of the guru—all of the mother
problems, father problems, anger, fear, anxiety, narcissism,
defenses, disdain. Everything. It all gets funneled into, acted
out through, and resolved with the guru.

Trungpa describes the progression of the relationship this
way: (He chooses to call the guru a spiritual friend here.)

> It has been said that the first stage of meeting one's spiritual
> friend is like going to a supermarket. You are excited and

you dream of all the different things that you are going to buy: the richness of your spiritual friend and the colorful qualities of his personality. The second stage of your relationship is like going to court, as though you were a criminal. You are not able to meet your friend's demands and you begin to feel self-conscious, because you know that he knows as much as you know about yourself, which is extremely embarrassing. In the third stage when you go to see your spiritual friend, it is like seeing a cow happily grazing in a meadow. You just admire its peacefulness and the landscape and then you pass on. Finally the fourth stage with one's spiritual friend is like passing a rock in the road. You do not even pay attention to it; you just pass by and walk away.[14]

This sounds very much to me like the way Kopp works. To his patients he becomes, for a while, almost all there is. Everything gets funneled into the relationship, acted out through it, and resolved in it. As the patient's attachments drop away this lessens until, toward termination time, like the spiritual friend, Kopp becomes the rock that gets passed by unnoticed.

Is this technique the most conducive for incorporating the spiritual dimension in the therapeutic setting? Is the guru, in fact, doing insight-oriented analytic work founded on a highly charged transference relationship? If so, wouldn't it make sense to adopt this Eastern model—one that already integrates the psychological and spiritual dimensions—in doing spiritually oriented psychotherapy? And most important, is there some part of the work—perhaps the spiritual, ego-relinquishing aspect—that can *only* be done this way? I don't know the answers to these questions. At the moment, I suspect that the answers are all yes. But they at least all merit a closer look.

I'm imagining (maybe just my hybris showing) a variety of people in the helping professions reading this chapter and wondering where they fit, or if they fit, or if they'd even *want* to fit. Which therapeutic approaches permit incorporating the spiritual dimension into the work and which don't?

Because the journey is both cognitive and affective, spiritual growth is inhibited in therapies that shortchange one or the other side. Therapies based entirely on ego psychology preclude spiritual deepening altogether. Client-centered, gestalt, and analytic therapies seem very amenable to embracing the spiritual dimension of the journey, but then my knowledge of the many and various contemporary humanistic approaches is limited.

The work I do is basically analytic insight-oriented psychotherapy incorporating the approach developed by Robert Langs as I learned it through Sheldon Kopp. It seems possible so far in my practice to incorporate the spiritual dimension comfortably, as, I hope, the anecdotes on the previous pages demonstrate. It will be interesting to see how things develop.

What about people who do nonanalytic work? What about supportive therapists, pastoral counselors, peer counselors, or family therapists? My guess is that the depth of the work doesn't matter much. It's the orientation that counts. It's always possible to view a patient or client as "a beneficial presence in the world." It's always possible for therapists or counselors to transcend their egos and love the people they work with. Regardless of how deep a swipe is taken through the dark valley, it can be a spiritual swipe.

This book is subtitled "Healing Journeys of Gay Christians" and I've tried throughout to pin the journey back down to a Christian context. In talking about the healer, I feel the need to make a Christian connection again.

I have always been moved by the vision of Jesus as the divine healer. Although I can't go the whole nine yards with Mary Baker Eddy, I've always thought the Christian Scientists had put their finger on something important. Jesus was some kind of therapist. He was the epitome of a professional lover. . What's more, he seemed especially effective when ministering to those "despised and rejected of men." Although scripture never quotes Jesus as saying *anything* about homosexual people, he did spend a lot of time with social outcasts. He also didn't mince any words about the poor and oppressed.

His attitude toward those rejected by society was always one of incredible compassion—empathy and unconditional positive regard. He identified with them, accepted their lot as his own, and loved them as they had never been loved before. He embraced them as beautiful expressions of the Creator's love, integral parts of salvation history. When they came to know and believe how much he loved them, they were overwhelmed—and healed. His impact on those people who knew him personally and on us who are their descendants was and is incalculable. To be loved by love, to come to know and believe that, is to create the same sort of excruciatingly joyful havoc at a cosmic level that I experienced during that eventful session with my therapist. Jesus made people know of their goodness so dramatically and so uncompromisingly that we came to recognize him as love itself, the Christ, begotten of God.

Only to the extent that therapists (whether or not they are Christian) can be Christlike vehicles of God's love can healing happen. Only to the degree that the therapist can see the reflection of Christ in all people can the Christhood of any patient be called forth.

Into the Lion's Den

"Love them anyway?" I moaned. "But how?"

"You begin by just being who you are," God said, "a loving, caring, whole person created in my image, whose special light of love happens to shine on men, as I intended for you."

"Is that all?" I asked fearfully.

God shook his head, "No, you must also speak your pain and affirm the wholeness I've made you to be when they assail it. You must protest when you are treated as less than a child of mine."

"Is there more?" I asked.

"Yes," God said gently, "and this is the hardest part of all. You must go out and teach them. Help them to know of their dependence on me for all that they really are, and of their helplessness without me. Teach them that their ways are not my ways, and that the world of their imagining is not the world I have made. Help them to see that all creation is one as I am one, and that all I create I redeem. And assure them by word and work and example that my love is boundless, and that I am with them always."

"You know they won't listen to me," I said with resignation. "They'll despise me. They'll call me a heretic and laugh me to scorn. They'll persecute and torment me. They'll try to destroy me. You know they will, don't you."

The radiant face saddened. And then God said softly, "O, yes. I know. How well I know."

I heard his words and something irrevocable changed in me. I went numb. Now I knew. Now I understood. And it was as though large chunks of who I had been began falling away, tumbling through time and space into eternity. I just let them all fall. No fear now. No resistance. No sense of loss. All that was dropping away was unnecessary now. Extraneous.

I began to feel light and warm. Energy began to surge through my whole being, enlivening me, as though I were a rusty old turbine that had been charged up and was starting to hum.

Then two strong, motherly arms reached out and drew me close to the bosom of all that is. And I was just there. Just being. Enveloped in being.

And we wept.

For joy.

Notes

Chapter 1 : *Once upon a Time*
1. Jas. 1:17 (N.E.B.)
2. Mt. 10:8 (N.A.B.)
3. Mt. 5:15–16 (N.E.B.)

Chapter 2 : *The Cleaving of the Soul*
1. To a lesser degree, there was a much more integrated view of the *whole* person, including the body.
2. Alan Watts, *Psychotherapy: East and West* (New York: Vintage Books, Random House, Inc., 1975).
3. Ibid.
4. The current "holistic health" movement carries the attempt at integration a step further to try to reunite mind, body, and soul.
5. Robert Langs, *The Technique of Psychoanalytic Psychotherapy*, vol. I (New York: Jason Aronson, Inc., 1973).
6. This whole concept of correcting patients' "maps of the universe" is treated well in Richard Bandler and John Grinder, *The Structure of Magic*, vol. I: *A Book about Language and Therapy* (Palo Alto, Calif.: Science and Behavior Books, Inc., 1975).
7. Evelyn Underhill, *Mysticism: A Study in the Nature and Development of Man's Spiritual Consciousness* (New York: E. P. Dutton & Co., Inc., 1961), pp. 413–443.
8. Psalm 8:4 (J.B.)
9. Thomas Merton, *The Seven Storey Mountain* (Garden City, N.Y.: Image Books, Doubleday & Company, Inc., 1970).
10. Underhill, *Mysticism*, pp. 198–231.

Chapter 3 : *The Enthronement of the Ego and the Myth*
1. Watts, *Psychotherapy*, pp. 21–44.
2. Paul Tillich, *Systematic Theology*, vol. I (Chicago: University of Chicago Press, 1951), p. 191.

Chapter 4 : *The Gay Predicament*
1. Howard Brown, *Familiar Faces, Hidden Lives: The Story of Homosexual Men in America Today* (New York: Harcourt Brace Jovanovich, 1976).
2. Ibid., p. 81.
3. John Bright, *A History of Israel*, 2nd ed. (Philadelphia: Westminster Press, 1972), pp. 343–373.
4. Is. 40:1–2 (N.E.B.)
5. Is. 40:12–15 (N.E.B.)
6. Is. 42:6–7 (N.E.B.)

Chapter 5 : *The Pain, the Pain*
1. Sheldon [B.] Kopp, quoted by Alison Cheek during a psychotherapy session.
2. Albert Ellis, *Humanistic Psychotherapy: The Rational-Emotive Approach* (New York: Julian Press, Inc., 1973), p. 56.
3. B. F. Skinner, *About Behaviorism* (New York: Alfred A. Knopf, 1974), p. 8.
4. Arthur Janov, *The Primal Scream: Primal Therapy: The Cure for Neurosis,* (New York: Delta Books, Dell Publishing Co., Inc., 1970).
5. Daniel Casriel, *A Scream Away from Happiness* (New York: Grosset and Dunlap, 1972).
6. C. G. Jung, *The Undiscovered Self*, trans. R. F. C. Hull (Boston: Little, Brown and Company for The Atlantic Monthly Press, 1957), p. 36.

Chapter 6 : *Psychotherapy as Grieving*
1. Elisabeth Kubler-Ross, *On Death and Dying* (New York: Macmillan Publishing Co., Inc., 1969).
2. Kathryn Kuhlman, *I Believe in Miracles* (New York: Pyramid Books, Pyramid Communications, Inc., 1969).
3. Taken from a wonderful poster that features Sheldon Kopp's second "Laundry List of Eternal Truths" called "No Nirvana Without Samsara" (Washington, D.C.: Yes! Inc., 1978).
4. Sheldon Kopp, *An End to Innocence: Facing Life without Illusions* (New York: Macmillan Publishing Co., Inc., 1978).

5. [Baba] Ram Dass, *Remember: Be Here Now* (Boulder, Colorado: Hanuman Foundation, 1978; New York: Crown Publishing, distributors).

6. Thomas Hora, *Existential Metapsychiatry* (New York: Seabury Press, 1977), pp. 94–98.

Chapter 7 : *Spiritual Growth as Grieving*

1. Chögyam Trungpa, *Cutting through Spiritual Materialism*, ed. John Baker and Marvin Casper [Clear Light Series, ed. Samuel Bercholz] (Boulder, Colorado: Shambala Publications, Inc., 1973; New York: Random House, distributors), p. 47.

2. Ibid., p. 81.

3. [Baba] Ram Dass, *Journey of Awakening: A Meditator's Guidebook*, ed. Daniel Goleman with Dwarkanath Bonner and Ram Dev [Dale Borglum] (New York: Bantam Books, Inc., 1978), p. 156.

4. Trungpa, *Spiritual Materialism*, pp. 81, 84.

5. Ibid., p. 81.

6. Ibid., p. 37–38.

7. Ibid., p. 197.

Chapter 8 : *Grieving Gay*

1. Sheldon [B.] Kopp, "No Nirvana Without Samsara" (Washington, D.C.: Yes! Inc., 1978), a poster.

2. This is supposedly a quotation from Abraham Lincoln. I spotted it on a placard mounted on the front of an apartment building. The tenants were fighting the conversion of this low-rent apartment building into condominiums. I understand they won. At any rate, I've never been able to find where President Lincoln used the epithet. I assume it referred to something about the Civil War or the Emancipation Proclamation or both.

3. Jn. 18:36 (R.S.V.)

Chapter 9 : *Exile for All: An Invitation*

1. Gerald G. May, *Simply Sane: Stop Fixing Yourself and Start Really Living* (New York: Paulist Press, 1977), pp. 12–13.

2. Watts, *Psychotherapy*.

3. George Orwell, *1984*, with an Afterword by Eric Fromm (New York: Signet Classics, New American Library, Inc., 1949).

4. Alvin Toffler, *Future Shock* (New York: Random House, 1970).

5. Aldous Huxley, *Brave New World* (New York: Bantam Books, Inc., 1958).

6. Robert A. Heinlein, *Stranger in a Strange Land* (New York: Berkeley Publishing Corporation, 1968).

7. M. Barr and D. McGregor, "Where Is the Wonder," lyrics to a song made popular by Barbra Streisand included on a phonodisc entitled *My Name Is Barbra* (New York: Columbia Records, Inc., n.d.).

8. Mt. 18:3 (N.E.B.)

Chapter 10 : *Witches and Wizards*

1. [Baba] Ram Dass, *The Only Dance There Is: Talks Given at the Menninger Foundation, Topeka, Kansas, 1970, and at Spring Grove Hospital, Spring Grove, Maryland, 1972* (Garden City, N.Y.: Anchor Press of Doubleday & Company, Inc., 1974), p. 20.

2. *The American College Dictionary*, ed. C. L. Barnhart and Jesse Stern (1964), p. 393.

3. Carl R. Rogers and Barry Stevens, *Person to Person: The Problem of Being Human: A New Trend in Psychology* (Lafayette, Calif.: Real People Press, 1967), p. 94.

4. Robert R. Carkhuff, *Helping and Human Relations: A Primer for Lay and Professional Helpers*, vol. I (New York: Holt, Rinehart and Winston, Inc., 1969).

5. Much of the confusion about empathy arises because of a lack of distinction between an "empathic response," which literally means the response of a person has an empathic *attitude*, and "reflections of feelings," which is a *technique*. Rogers happens to believe that reflecting feelings back to patients is the *only* technique to be used in psychotherapy. So it was easy for people to confuse the empathic attitude he encourages with the technique. Most therapists don't agree with Rogers and use reflection of feelings as only *one* technique among many others. But most therapists still assume an empathic attitude to be essential, even when using techniques very different from reflection of feelings, like confrontation. For a clear discussion of the use of reflection of feelings, see Sheldon [B.] Kopp, *Back to One: A Practical Guide for Psychotherapists* (Palo Alto, Calif.: Science and Behavior Books, Inc., 1977), pp. 125–129.

6. Rogers and Stevens, *Person to Person*, p. 94.

7. May, *Simply Sane*, p. 130.

8. There is a fine but important point to note here. Taking patients as they are or "letting them be" is different from "accepting" them. There's an ego attachment in the word *accept*. It assumes the *right* to reject. From a spiritual perspective, that's a right we don't have. For a discussion of this, see Hora, *Metapsychiatry*, p. 69.

9. Watts, *Psychotherapy*, pp. 122–187.

10. M. Scott Peck, *The Road Less Travelled: A New Psychology of Love, Traditional Values and Spiritual Growth* (New York: Simon and Schuster, 1978), p. 81.

11. Sheldon [B.] Kopp, quoted by Alison Cheek during a psychotherapy session.

12. Hora, *Metapsychiatry*, p. 166.

13. Hora, *Metapsychiatry*, p. 139.

14. Trungpa, *Spiritual Materialism*, pp. 42–43.

Bibliography

Altman, Dennis. *Homosexual: Oppression and Liberation.* New York: Discus Books, Hearst Corporation, 1973.

Bandler, Richard, and Grinder, John. *The Structure of Magic.* Vol. I: *A Book about Language and Therapy.* Palo Alto, Calif.: Science and Behavior Books, Inc., 1975.

Bell, Alan P., and Weinberg, Martin S. *Homosexualities: A Study of Diversity among Men and Women.* New York: Simon and Schuster, 1978.

Breener, Charles. *An Elementary Textbook of Psychoanalysis.* New York: Anchor Books, 1974.

Brown, Howard. *Familiar Faces, Hidden Lives: The Story of Homosexual Men in America Today.* New York: Harcourt Brace Jovanovich, 1976.

Bulka, Reuven P., ed. *Mystics and Medics: A Comparison of Mystical and Psychotherapeutic Encounters.* New York: Human Sciences Press, 1979.

Bullough, Vern L. *Homosexuality: A History.* New York: Garland STPM Press, 1979; New American Library, 1979.

Clark, Don. *Loving Someone Gay.* Millibrae, Calif.: Celestial Arts, 1977.

Coster, Geraldine. *Yoga and Western Psychology: A Comparison.* New York: Harper Colophon Books, Harper & Row, Publishers, 1972.

Doherty, Catherine de Hueck. *Poustinia: Christian Spirituality of the East for Western Man.* Notre Dame, Ind.: Ave Maria Press, 1975.

Ebner, James H. *God Present as Mystery: A Search for Personal Meaning in Contemporary Theology.* Winona, Minn.: St. Mary's College Press, 1978.

Edwards, Tilden. *Living Simply through the Day: Spiritual Survival in a Complex Age.* New York: Paulist Press, 1977.

Fisher, Peter. *The Gay Mystique: The Myth and Reality of Male Homosexuality.* New York: Day Books, Stein and Day, Publishers, 1978.

Fox, Matthew. *On Becoming a Musical, Mystical Bear: Spirituality American Style.* New York: Paulist Press, 1976.

———. *WHEE! We, Wee All the Way Home: A Guide to the New Sensual Spirituality.* n.p.: Consortium Books, 1976.

Gearhart, Sally, and Johnson, William R. *Loving Women/Loving Men: Gay Liberation and the Church.* San Francisco: Glide Publications, 1974.

Golas, Thaddeus. *The Lazy Man's Guide to Enlightenment.* Palo Alto, Calif.: Seed Center, 1972.

Grinder, John, and Bandler, Richard. *The Structure of Magic.* Vol. II. Palo Alto, Calif.: Science and Behavior Books, Inc., 1976.

Haley, Jay. *Strategies of Psychotherapy.* New York: Grune and Stratton, Inc., 1963.

———. *Uncommon Therapy: The Psychiatric Techniques of Milton Erickson, M.D.* New York: W. W. Norton and Company, Inc., 1973.

Heinlein, Robert A. *Stranger in a Strange Land.* New York: Berkeley Publishing Corporation, 1961.

Hora, Thomas. *Existential Metapsychiatry.* New York: Seabury Press, 1977.

Huxley, Aldous. *Brave New World.* New York: Bantam Books, Inc., 1958.

In Praise of Krishna: Songs from the Bengali. Translated by Edward C. Dimock, Jr. and Denise Levertov. Introduction and Notes by Edward C. Dimock, Jr. Garden City, N.Y.: Anchor Books, Doubleday & Company, Inc., 1967.

James, William. *The Varieties of Religious Experience: A Study in Human Nature.* New York: Longmans, Green, and Co., 1912.

Jay, Karla, and Young, Allen. *The Gay Report: Lesbians and Gay Men Speak Out About Sexual Experiences and Lifestyles.* New York: Summit Books, 1979.

Johnston, William. *Christian Zen.* New York: Harper Colophon Books, Harper & Row, Publishers, 1971.

Jones, Clinton R. *Understanding Gay Relatives and Friends.* New York: Seabury Press, 1978.

Journal of Homosexuality. Edited by Charles Silverstein, Ph.D. New York: Haworth Press, 1975– .

Jung, C. G. *The Undiscovered Self.* Translated by R. F. C. Hull. Boston:

Atlantic Monthly Press Book, Little, Brown and Company, 1958.

Kopp, Sheldon B. *Back to One: A Practical Guide for Psychotherapists.* Palo Alto, Calif.: Science and Behavior Books, 1977.

———. *An End to Innocence: Facing Life without Illusions.* New York: Macmillan Publishing Co., Inc., 1978.

———. *Guru: Metaphors from a Psythotherapist.* Palo Alto, Calif.: Science and Behavior Books, Inc., 1971.

———. *If you Meet the Buddha on the Road, Kill Him!: The Pilgrimage of Psychotherapy Patients.* New York: Bantam Books, 1972.

Kubler-Ross, Elisabeth. *On Death and Dying.* New York: Macmillan Publishing Co., Inc., 1969.

Langs, Robert. *The Listening Process.* New York: Jason Aronson, 1978.

———. *The Technique of Psychoanalytic Psychotherapy.* Vols. I and II. New York: Jason Aronson, Inc., 1973.

———, and Stone, Leo. *The Therapeutic Experience and Its Setting: A Dialogue.* New York: Jason Aronson, Inc., 1980.

McNeill, John J. *The Church and the Homosexual.* Kansas City: Sheed Andrews & McMeel, Inc., 1976.

Martin, Del, and Lyon, Phyllis. *Lesbian/Woman.* New York: Bantam Books, Inc., 1972.

May, Gerald G. *Pilgrimage Home: The Conduct of Contemplative Practice in Groups.* New York: Paulist Press, 1979.

———. *Simply Sane: Stop Fixing Yourself and Start Really Living.* New York: Paulist Press, 1977.

Merton, Thomas. *Contemplative Prayer.* Garden City, N.Y.: Image Books, Doubleday & Company, Inc., 1971.

———. *No Man Is an Island.* Garden City, N.Y.: Image Books, Doubleday & Company, Inc., 1967.

———. *Selected Poems of Thomas Merton.* Enlarged Edition. Introduction by Mark Van Doren. New York: New Directions Publishing Corporation for James Laughlin, 1967.

———. *The Seven Storey Mountain.* Garden City, N.Y.: Image Books, Doubleday & Company, Inc., 1970.

———. *The Sign of Jonas.* Garden City, N.Y.: Image Books, Doubleday & Company, Inc., 1956.

———. *Thoughts in Solitude.* Garden City, N.Y.: Image Books, Doubleday & Company, Inc., 1968.

Nelson, James B. *Embodiment: An Approach to Sexuality and Christian Theology.* Minneapolis, Minn.: Augsburg Publishing House, 1978.

Nouwen, Henri J. M. *Reaching Out: The Three Movements of the Spiritual Life.* Garden City, N.Y.: Doubleday & Company, Inc., 1975.

Peck, M. Scott. *The Road Less Travelled: A New Psychology of Love, Traditional Values and Spiritual Growth.* New York: Simon and Schuster, 1978.

Perls, Frederick S. *Gestalt Therapy Verbatim.* Compiled and edited by John O. Stevens. Lafayette, Calif.: Real People Press, 1969.

———. *In and Out of the Garbage Pail.* Moab, Utah: Real People Press, 1969.

———. Hefferline, Ralph E., and Goodman, Paul. *Gestalt Therapy.* New York: Delta Books, Dell Publishing Co., Inc., 1951.

Pittenger, Norman. *Gay Lifestyles: A Christian Interpretation of Homosexuality and the Homosexual.* Los Angeles: Universal Fellowship Press, 1977.

———. *Time for Consent.* London: SMC Press, Ltd., 1970.

Ram Dass. *Journey of Awakening: A Meditator's Guidebook.* Edited by Daniel Goleman with Dwarkanath Bonner and Ram Dev (Dale Borglum). New York: Bantam Books, Inc., 1978.

———. *Miracle of Love: Stories about Neem Karoli Baba.* New York: E. P. Dutton, 1979.

———. *The Only Dance There Is: Talks Given at the Menninger Foundation, Topeka, Kansas, 1970, and at Spring Grove Hospital, Spring Grove, Maryland, 1972.* Garden City, N.Y.: Anchor Press of Doubleday, Publishers, 1974.

———. *Remember: Be Here Now.* Boulder, Colorado: Hanuman Foundation, 1978.

Reich, Wilhelm. *Character-Analysis.* 3rd ed. New York: Orgone Institute Press, 1949.

Rice, Edward. *The Man in the Sycamore Tree: The Good Time and Hard Life of Thomas Merton: An Entertainment with Photographs.* Garden City: N.Y.: Image Books, Doubleday & Company, Inc., 1972.

Rogers, Carl R. *Client-Centered Therapy: Its Current Practice, Implications and Theory.* With chapters contributed by Elaine Dorfman, Thomas Gordon, and Nicholas Hobbs. Boston: Houghton Mifflin Company, 1965.

———. *On Becoming a Person: A Therapist's View of Psychotherapy.* Boston: Houghton Mifflin Company, 1961.

———, and Stevens, Barry. *Person to Person: The Problem of Being Human: A New Trend in Psychology.* With contributions by Eugene T. Gendlin, John M. Shlien, and Wilson Van Dusen. Lafayette, Calif.: Real People Press, 1967.

Ross, Nancy Wilson. *Three Ways of Asian Wisdom: Hinduism, Buddhism, Zen and Their Significance for the West*. New York: Clarion Books, Simon and Schuster, 1966.

Salzman, Leon, M.D. *The Obsessive Personality: Origins, Dynamics, and Therapy*. Rev. ed. New York: Jason Aronson, Inc., 1973.

Santideva. *Entering the Path of Enlightenment: The Bodhicaryavatara of the Buddhist Poet Santideva*. Translation with guide by Marion L. Matics. New York: Macmillan Company, 1970; London: Collier-Macmillan Ltd., 1970.

Shapiro, David. *Neurotic Styles*. Foreword by Robert P. Knight. Austen Riggs Center Monograph Series Number 5. New York: Basic Books, Inc., 1965.

Silverstein, Charles. *A Family Matter: A Parents' Guide to Homosexuality*. New York: McGraw-Hill Book Company, 1977.

Squire, Aelred. *Asking the Fathers: The Art of Meditation and Prayer*. Wilton, Conn.: Morehouse-Barlow Co., Inc., 1973; New York: Paulist Press, 1973.

Storm, Hyemeyohsts. *Seven Arrows*. New York: Ballantine Books, 1972.

Sullivan, Harry Stack. *Clinical Studies in Psychiatry*. Edited by Helen Swick Perry, Mary Ladd Gawel, and Martha Gibbon. Foreword by Dexter M. Bullard. New York: W. W. Norton & Company, Inc., 1956.

Trungpa, Chogyam. *Cutting through Spiritual Materialism*. Edited by John Baker and Marvin Casper. Clear Light Series. Boulder Colorado: Shambhala Publications, Inc., 1973.

Ulanov, Ann, and Ulanov, Barry. *Religion and the Unconscious*. Philadelphia: Westminster Press, 1975.

Underhill, Evelyn. *Mysticism: A Study in the Nature and Development of Man's Spiritual Consciousness*. New York: E. P. Dutton, 1961.

Voices: The Art and Science of Psychotherapy: Journal of the American Academy of Psychotherapists. Edited by E. Mark Stern. New York: American Academy of Psychotherapists, 1978– .

Watts, Alan. *Psychotherapy: East and West*. New York: Vintage Books, Random House, 1975.

Weinberg, George. *Society and the Healthy Homosexual*. New York: Anchor Press of Doubleday Publishers, 1973.

Weinberg, Martin S., and Williams, Colin J. *Male Homosexuals: Their Problems and Adaptations*. New York: Oxford University Press, 1974.